1 MONTH OF
FREE
READING

at

www.ForgottenBooks.com

By purchasing this book you are eligible for one month membership to ForgottenBooks.com, giving you unlimited access to our entire collection of over 1,000,000 titles via our web site and mobile apps.

To claim your free month visit:

www.forgottenbooks.com/free913782

ISBN 978-0-266-94600-7
PIBN 10913782

This book is a reproduction of an important historical work. Forgotten Books uses state-of-the-art technology to digitally reconstruct the work, preserving the original format whilst repairing imperfections present in the aged copy. In rare cases, an imperfection in the original, such as a blemish or missing page, may be replicated in our edition. We do, however, repair the vast majority of imperfections successfully; any imperfections that remain are intentionally left to preserve the state of such historical works.

A History

of

First Baptist Church

Dunn, North Carolina

1885-1981

BY:

HERMAN P. GREEN

AUGUST 31, 1981

Library of Congress Catalog Card No. 81-71423

Sponsor: First Baptist Church
West Broad Street at Layton Avenue
Dunn, North Carolina 28334

Printed in The United States of America
By: Twyford Printing Company, Dunn, N. C.

TABLE OF CONTENTS

Div.Sch.
286
.1756362
G796
H673
1981

3

In a regular Deacons Meeting of the First Baptist Church held January 8, 1979, upon recommendation of the Pastor, Dr. Thomas M. Freeman, the Diaconate commissioned me to write a history of this Church and the action was confirmed in a regular church conference on January 10, 1979. This I have made an honest effort to do. Temptation has been great at times to insert into this work many valuable events told to me that probably are true and correct. However, we realize that all memories play tricks at times. Also that events passed down from "mouth to ear" do in some cases become unintentionally distorted. However, I believe that all histories and especially Church histories should be truly factual and unbiased. I, therefore, determined at the very outset not to include anything that could not be documented or authenticated. This I have done except in one small instance where circumstantial evidence to me justified the risk.

To the custodians of the records mentioned in the bibliography and to the many others who furnished "pointers" or who extended encouragement, when frustration became evident, because the failure to obtain records led so often to "dead end streets" I extend most heartfelt thanks. To Mrs. Joseph C. (Emma Ann) Ruark, who so freely and without restraint, allowed me access to all the writings both Churchwise and Secular of her father, Herbert B. Taylor, and allowed me to photograph in her home two items described in this history, I express my most sincere appreciation.

To George W. Williams, Church Clerk, to Dr. Thomas M. Freeman, Pastor, to Rev. Ray Phillips, Minister of Music and Education and to Mrs. Wesley (Ruth) Fowler, Church Secretary, I owe a debt of gratitude for their assistance; to Dr. Gary L. Josey, who assumed responsibility for the typing and Ms. Carolyn Mills, who so patiently and skillfully typed this work from my handwritten manuscript and put it in form for the printers, I want to express my thanks for a job so unselfishly done.

To my devoted wife, Elizabeth, who proofed the manuscript and who said "Don't stop now!" when so many times circumstances tempted me to quit. It takes much spirited cooperation to accomplish such tasks.

By a Resolution of this Church Diaconate passed on the 8th day of January, 1979 and confirmed in a regular church conference on January 10, 1979, this writer was commissioned to search out the historical truth wherever and whenever it may be found and to so record it as a history of the First Baptist Church of Dunn, N. C. That task is now finished and, I fear, in a very imperfect manner. I, there, return all records to the places from whence they came with the earnest hope that the members of this Church and others who read this work will make due allowance for all errors that may have been committed, with the assurance that whatever duties which, as a Church member, have been placed upon me, that my zeal as a Christian Layman has always prompted me to do the very best I can.

HERMAN P. GREEN

FOREWORD

The history of a church is the story of God and His people working and ministering together in a local community. It cannot be told routinely, nor properly told by an outsider. It requires faith in God, love for His people, a deep interest and a willingness to search and work so that the whole story can be handed down to succeeding generations.

Herman Patrick Green has proved to be an ideal church historian, for he is and has been for many years an active member of the Dunn First Baptist Church and a vital part of its ministry in the community. At the same time he has been a man of deep faith, of great love for the Lord and His people, and a person who appreciates and is interested in both secular and sacred history.

But it has been his willingness to research the history of the Dunn First Baptist Church, and his determination to produce a complete and accurate story of its life, that has made possible the whole story. He has spent more hours than even he has counted, driven his car more miles than he has recorded, and worked more hours in devoted writing and rewriting than any of us realize. He has done this as a labor of love, without any desire for praise or remuneration, and it has resulted in one of the most complete, reliable and interesting church histories that I have ever read.

Not only does the Dunn First Baptist Church owe a great deal to Herman Patrick Green for this splendid history, but past generations and future generations are also in his debt. I felt that it ought not to be printed without this tribute of appreciation to him.

Dr. Thomas M. Freeman, Pastor

Chapter I

Organization
and Early History

The ordeal of the bloody "War Between The States" came to an end on April 26, 1865. Families in eastern Harnett County, as elsewhere, had begun to pick up the pieces and put their lives together. The Averasboro Battlefield so near and the Bentonville Battlefield not too far away are two of many places where brave and faithful men sacrificed for causes those on each side believed to be true and right. The Chicora Cemetery where rest at least 54 Confederate dead, 52 of which are unidentified "unknown soldiers" is visible evidence of such sacrifice.

Continued search for religious truth was a major factor in this rebuilding process. The South River Baptist Association and probably other associations were sending out "roving missionaries". These missionaries were to preach and witness to groups wherever they could be assembled and to form churches when suitable interest and genuine enthusiasm were evident.

As evidence that this movement began very early after the "war" there is quoted below part of an article found on Page 16 of South River Baptist Association Minutes of 1893.

"The origin of 'Antioch' Church in Cumberland County may be traced back to the times before the 'War Between The States' when Elder A. B. Alderman, a most faithful and diligent servant of God, commenced preaching in the vicinity of the present Church about the year 1858 and was about to begin the work of building a house of worship when the war came on and the people left their homes for the field of carnage."

"After that great struggle ended the Executive Board of the 'Cedar Creek Association' sent Rev. J. M. Beasley, another active and earnest worker in the Lord's vineyard to that field, and with his abundant means and also by the help of a few of the brethren, the House was built, and in May, 1869, Antioch was organized with twenty-six members; they elected Elder J. M. Beasley as pastor, who served the Church in that office till 1876."

It may be interesting to note here that Rev. Sam F. Hudson also served for a period as pastor of this Antioch Church. Rev. Sam Hudson is now a retired pastor after many years of fruitful service and is a member of this Church.

There is evidence that in 1883 one or more of "South River Association Roving Missionaries" was preaching in

Pope's Schoolhouse in Harnett County. The name of this schoolhouse was later changed to Greenwood Schoolhouse. Efforts in this area began to bear fruit and to produce visible evidence. Part of an article appearing in the Bibical Recorder of Wednesday, October 21, 1885, written by Elder S. C. Page is copied below:

"CHURCH ORGANIZED"

"At the request of certain brethren and sisters a Presbytery consisting of Elders H. J. Duncan, W. R. Johnson, and the writer with brother H. L. Hall, W. Royal and J. B. Downing from the Mission Board of the South River Association, as an advisory council, met on the twenty-seventh of September at Greenwood School House, Harnett County. This point has been occupied by the Board of South River Association for some time. It being decided that the time had come to organize a Church at this place the Presbytery organized by calling Rev. H. J. Duncan to the chair and Bro. J. B. Downing as Secretary. Five members came with letters from other Churches and six came forward who had been baptized by Rev. W. R. Johnson, the present Missionary, making it eleven in all. After adopting a suitable covenant and constitution they received the right hand of fellowship by the Presbytery and were pronounced in a regular Baptist Church by the name of Greenwood."

Thus we have an article printed in the Bibical Recorder just twenty-four days after Greenwood Church was organized, written by a member of the organizing Presbytery or advisory council giving the exact date of organization, the exact number of charter members and the full list of the advisory council sent out by the Mission Board of the South River Association for the purpose of organizing the Greenwood Church on the fourth Sunday in September, 1885.

In the minutes of the South River Association Meeting of October, 1893, there is printed on Pages 16-19 an article entitled:

"A History in Part of the 'South River' Baptist Association" together with accounts of the origin of a few of the Churches that first united in the organization known as the South River Association of regular or "missionary Baptists".

Some of this article gives additional information on the organization of the Greenwood Church and, therefore, sections appearing on parts of Pages 16 and 17 are quoted below:

"The Baptist Church at Dunn, had its beginning before the railroad whistle was heard waking the echoes in the pine forests of the southern corner of Harnett County, where the little city of 800 or more inhabitants, and its six Churches now stand on the line of railroad between Wilson and Fayetteville."

"In the year 1884, the Executive Board of the South River Association at their meeting at Salem Church in December, 1883, authorized Rev. A. B. Alderman to visit Pope's School-House, in Harnett County, and preach as opportunity afforded. He did so, and kept up a regular appointment there until the following August, reporting to the Board at their August meeting that Pope's School House was an important point and prospects there encouraging. Pope's School-House is the place known as the Greenwood School-House and is about a mile beyond the present corporate limits of the town of Dunn; a place that had no existance at that time. For his services at Pope's School-House that year, Bro. Alderman was paid $22.50."

"The next year, 1885, Elder W. R. Johnson was employed by the Executive Board to take up the work at Greenwood School-House which he did, holding a meeting of days there, being assisted by Elder W. M. Page, and having baptized six persons, a Presbytery was called, composed of Elders W. R. Johnson, H. J. Duncan and S. C. Page, with Bro. J. B. Downing, Clerk, and H. L. Hall, Assistant Clerk, who organized and recognized the following persons, who presented themselves with letters of dismission and certificates of Baptism, into a regular missionary Baptist Church, known as the Greenwood Baptist Church of Harnett County, N. C. The names of the brethren and sisters are as follows: Wm. H. Pope, E. C. Pope, L. G. Dorman, J. M. Jones, A. J. Stanley, J. C. Godwin, Elizabeth Pope, Emily Pope, Sarah W. Jones, Winnfred Byrd and E. J. Godwin."

"The Church thus organized resolved to unite with the South River Association, and delegates were at once appointed, namely: Wm. H. Pope, E. C. Pope and J. M. Jones. Elder W. R. Johnson was elected Pastor of the Church, and continued to serve them through 1885, 1886 and 1887." Thus we have here the names of the eleven charter members. We also have repeated the names of the organizing Presbytery or Advisory Council.

The Ninth Annual Session of the South River Association met with the Church at Magnolia, Cumberland County, N.

C., October 20, 21, and 22, 1885. On the first morning of the meeting, October 20, 1885, page five of the minutes has recorded thereon the following:

"Called for petitionary letters, when the Church at Greenwood, Harnett County, (newly constituted) presented her petitionary letter. On motion the Church was received and the following enrolled as messengers: Wm. H. Pope and E. C. Pope and the right hand of fellowship given them by the moderator."

We note here that only twenty three days after the Greenwood Church was organized and one day before the article referred to above was printed in the Bibical Recorder, the Greenwood Church was officially received into membership of the South River Association. It also may be of interest to know that this Church was the only Church from Harnett County at that time to be a member of the South River Association and remained the only Church in Harnett County to be a member of that Association until it affiliated with the Little River Association.

The minutes of the Eleventh Annual Session of the South River Association held October, 1887, continues to list this Church as "Greenwood" and the Church letter to the Association lists its membership as nine males and twelve females or a total of twenty-one. The minutes, however, of the Twelfth Annual Session of the South River Association held October 24, 25 and 26, 1888, shows the name had been changed in the meantime from "Greenwood Baptist Church" to "Dunn Baptist Church" and the Church letter listed its membership of twelve males and twenty-two females or a total of thirty-four.

The Thirteenth Annual Session of the South River Association met October 23, 24 and 25, 1889, at the Dunn Baptist Church, Harnett County, N.C. The Church letter to the Association at that time listed its membership as twenty-nine males and thrity females or a total of fifty-nine.

The Fifteenth Annual Session of the South River Association in October, 1891, listed a membership of the Dunn Church at thirty-eight males and fifty-two females or ninety members. The minutes of this session also listed for the first time a Sunday school at the Dunn Church consisting of eight teachers and fifty-seven pupils and R. G. Taylor as the Superintendent. However, there is very strong and compelling evidence that the Sunday school was organized in 1888 and that Sam Parker was its Superintendent for the first three years.

In a regular Church conference held October 15, 1893, the delegates from this Church to the South River Association to be held in a few days were instructed to ask for a letter of dismissal from that association in order for this Church to join the Little River Association.

In another Church conference held October 27, 1893, B. F. Campbell and E. T. Spence were elected as delegates to the Little River Association Annual Session to be held on November 2, 3, 4 and 5, 1893, at Mt. Tabor Baptist Church, Cumberland County, N. C., and were "instructed to carry our letter and ask to be connected with their body."

During the first day of the annual session of the Little River Association held at Mt. Tabor Baptist Church, Cumberland County, N. C., on November 2, 3, 4 and 5, 1893, a petition was submitted from the Dunn Baptist Church, Harnett County, N. C., requesting membership in Little River Association. This petition was granted and is so recorded on Page Four in the minutes of this session. The Dunn Baptist Church is recorded in the October, 1893, Annual Session Minutes of the South River Association as being one of its members but there is no mention of any kind of the Dunn Church in the minutes of the October, 1894, session of this Association.

It might be of some interest to note here that the Little River Association was organized at the Cumberland Union Baptist Church, Harnett County, N. C., in 1875 and that it held its first annual session on November 2, 3, 4, 5, 1876, at the Lillington Baptist Church, Harnett County, N. C.

It also might be of some interest to mention here that the Town of Dunn was incorporated under private laws of 1887 Chapter 23 and ratified February 12, 1887. The town was laid out in the form of a circle with a radius of one-half mile (2640 feet). An iron buggy axle was driven equidistant between the rails of the railroad southbound main track in the exact center of Broad Street to mark the center of the circle.

Chapter II

Real Estate
Transactions

Real estate transactions are an important part of any Church activity. They establish roots and point to progress and dreams realized. The First Baptist Church of Dunn has thus far entered into or been a part of twenty-one such transactions of various kinds.

The first such activity was for the purchase of a lot in Dunn for the purpose of erecting its first Church thereon. The deed is dated June 1, 1887, and was from Henry Pope and wife Eliza Pope (grantors) to James A. Taylor and others, Trustees of First Baptist Church (grantee). Part of the deed reads "in consideration of fifty dollars to them paid by the parties of the second part---." The description of the real estate reads "beginning at alley on Broad Street thence said street 140 feet to Layton Street thence down said Layton Street 150 ft. thence back to alley 140 ft. thence up said alley 150 ft. to beginning on Broad Street and is know as Baptist Church lot."

This deed was first recorded in Book W on Page 288, Harnett County Registry. The book was destroyed in the courthouse fire and it was later re-recorded in Book 415 on Page 472 Harnett County Registry on January 2, 1963. This, of course, is the lot on which the present building stands.

There is an interesting sidelight concerning this instrument. It is made to "First Baptist Church". The official name at that time was Dunn Baptist Church and was not changed to First Baptist Church until about 1909.

The second transaction is a mortgage deed dated April 18, 1888, from First Baptist Church (grantor) to Jake Beasley (grantee) and is recorded in Book L-1 on Page 121 Harnett County Registry. The amount of the loan was five hundred seventy-five dollars and was used in constructing the first or Wooden Church house. The property mortgaged is the same lot described in the first instrument mentioned above.

Two sidelights could be pointed out here. First, the grantor is "First Baptist Church". Second, this mortgage deed remains still uncanceled of record. This, however, is of no real importance to the title since many years ago the Statute of Limitations took effect.

We find for the third activity a deed dated May 8, 1909, recorded in Book 170 on Page 491 Harnett County Registry from P. T. Massengill and wife Elvira Massengill (grantors) to Dunn Baptist Church (grantee). The consideration was "one hundred ten dollars to them paid by parties of the second part---". This lot was approximately 100 ft. x 150 ft. and is located on the southeast corner of what is now the intersection of South Magnolia Avenue and East Duke Street.

The "South Dunn Baptist Church" was organized by the First Baptist Church and occupied a building erected on this lot for that purpose. Disposition of this lot by the First Baptist Church fourteen years later is set forth in Item Six below.

Item Number Four is a deed of trust dated May 14, 1914, and recorded in Book 109 on Pages 134 and 135 Harnett County Registry from First Baptist Church, Dunn, N. C., part of the first part, to Southern Life and Trust Company of Greensboro, N. C., party of the second part, Southern Underwriters of Greensboro, N. C., and Dunn Insurance & Realty Company, Dunn, N. C., parties of the third part. The amount of the loan was $10,000.00 payable in five annual installments of $2,000.00 on the 14th day of May in the years 1916, 1917, 1918, 1919 and 1920. Interest was at the rate of six percent payable semi-annually.

The purpose of this loan was to pay off part of the debts accumulated in the construction of the present brick Church. The real estate securing this loan was that lot described in Item One above plus "a certain policy or policies of insurance hereinafter designated shall be assigned as collateral security as hereinafter set out." This deed of trust was canceled of record November 19, 1919.

The next real estate transaction, Number Five, is a deed dated December 31, 1921, recorded in Book 196 on Page 554 from Arthur F. Pope and wife Will Cooper Pope (grantors) to First Baptist Church, Dunn, N. C. (grantees). This house and lot fronts on the west side of South Layton Avenue between West Divine Street and West Pearsall Street. The lot is 75 ft. x 140 ft. and the address is 308 South Layton Avenue. This is the first parsonage owned by the First Baptist Church and remained its property for about twenty-five years.

Item Six is a deed dated March 30, 1923, recorded in Book 199 on page 317 Harnett County Registry from First Baptist Church, Dunn, N. C. (grantor) to Cassie Hodges "in consideration of two thousand dollars to him paid by party of the second part". This is the same lot described in Item Three above.

Transaction Number Seven is a deed of trust dated March 30, 1923, from B. A. Hodges and wife Cassie Hodges (grantors) to First Baptist Church. The amount of the indebtedness was fifteen hundred dollars "bearing interest from date at six percent per annum and due and payable as follows: $500.00 due January 1, 1924; $500.00 due January 1, 1925, and $500.00 due January 1, 1926." This is the same lot described in Item Three above. This deed of trust was canceled of record April 25, 1927.

The Number Eight Item is a deed dated April 14, 1945, and recorded in Book 295 on Page 165 Harnett County Registry from L. A. Tart and wife Martha R. Tart (grantors) to First Baptist Church, Dunn, N. C. (grantee) "in consideration of three thousand and no/100 dollars to them paid by the parties of the second part---". This lot is 75 ft. fronting on South Layton Avenue and 150 ft. on West Cumberland Street and is the lot on which the present parsonage is situated.

The Ninth instrument is a deed dated April 18, 1945, by N. M. Johnson and wife Bessie D. Johnson (grantors) to First Baptist Church (grantee) and is recorded in Book 294 on Page 185 Harnett County Registry. This is the parsonage lot described in instrument Eight above. "The purpose of this deed is that the grantors desire to release and quitclaim to the grantees and their assigns any interest which the grantors might have in the above described tract of land."

Instrument Number Ten is a deed dated August 15, 1946, recorded in Book 302 on Page 153 Harnett County from First Baptist Church, Dunn, N. C. (grantor) to Mrs. Sally Cooper. Part of the deed reads as follows: "in consideration of ten thousand and no/100 dollars to it paid by the party of the second part---". This is the same lot described in Item Five above.

The Eleventh transaction is a deed dated March 30, 1953, from Ottis Jackson and wife Doris Jackson to First Baptist Church, Dunn, N. C., and is recorded in Book 345 on Page 177 Harnett County Registry. This lot is 75 ft. x 140 ft. and is located on the southwest corner of North Clinton Avenue and East Carr Street and is the lot on which North Clinton Avenue Baptist Church is now situated.

The Twelfth Instrument is a deed dated November 2, 1955, and recorded in Book 365 on Page 415 Harnett County Registry from Paul C. Hood, et. al, to First Baptist Church, Dunn, N. C. Part of the deed reads as follows: "that said parties of the first part in consideration of five thousand and no/100 dollars and other valuable considerations to them paid by said parties of the second part---". The size of this lot is 140 ft. x 150 ft. and is on the southwest corner of West Broad Street and South King Avenue. It is known by members of the Church as the "Hood property" on which the Sunday school annex building is situated.

The Thirteenth transaction was a deed of trust dated February 10, 1956, and recorded in Book 355 on Page 277 Harnett County Registry. The deed of trust was from First Baptist Church, Dunn, N.C., to Paul C. Hood, Helen H. Prince, Madrid H. Best and Thomas R. Hood. The amount of the indebtedness was "in the sum of fifteen thousand and no/100 dollars for balance of the purchase price for the lands hereinafter described." The interest rate was at six percent per annum. The property is the same as that described in Item Twelve above. This instrument has been canceled of record.

The Fourteenth Instrument is a deed dated August 15, 1960, from the First Baptist Church, Dunn, N. C., to North Clinton Avenue Baptist Church and recorded in Book 398 on Page 377 Harnett County Registry. Part of the deed is as follows: "for the further consideration of the sum of ten dollars, the receipt of which is hereby acknowledged----". This is the same property described in Item Number Eleven above.

Transaction Fifteen is a deed from Walter H. Adams, unmarried, to First Baptist Church, Dunn, N. C., dated November 1, 1963, and recorded in Book 440 on Page 5 Harnett County Registry. Part of the deed is as follows: "that the said Walter H. Adams, party of the first part, does hereby convey as 'a gift and charitable donation' to the trustees of the First Baptist Church, Dunn, N. C.----". This is a tract of land containing 6.89 acres and is on the old Coats Road (S.R. #1725) occupied now by Westfield Baptist Church.

The Sixteenth instrument is a deed from the First Baptist Church to Westfield Baptist Church dated July 22, 1964, and recorded in Book 452 on Page 141 Harnett County Registry. This is the same tract of land described in Item Fifteen above and was conveyed "for the further consideration of the sum of ten dollars---".

Item Seventeen is a deed of subordination dated September 5, 1966, between First Baptist Church, Dunn, N. C., party of the first part and Westfield Baptist Church, party of the second part. The tract of land involved is the same tract described in Items fifteen and sixteen above.

The deed in Item Sixteen above and a restriction in it to the effect that if the property ever was put to uses other than a missionary Baptist Church title to the property would automatically revert back to First Baptist Church, Dunn, N. C. Because of the restriction the deed of subordination reads in part as follows: "and whereas, said parties of the second part can procure a loan only upon condition that the first condition, that is, that the property shall only be used as a missionary Baptist Church, be waived, released and subordinated to the liens and deeds of trust executed and to be executed to certain lending institutions; and whereas, said parties of the first part have agreed to such saiver, release, and subordination, after being so authorized and directed by resolution passed by the First Baptist Church of Dunn, North Carolina, in regular Church conference assembled on Sunday night September 4, 1966----".

The Eighteenth transaction is a deed of trust dated January 27, 1969, and recorded in Book 512 on Page 91 Harnett County Registry. It was executed by First Baptist Church of Dunn, N. C., in favor of Home Savings and Loan Association of Dunn, N. C., for the purpose of obtaining a loan from said Association in the amount of one hundred five thousand dollars. The property described in this deed of trust is the same property referred to in Item Twelve above (Hood property). The funds obtained by this transaction was used in the construction of the Sunday school annex situated on this lot. This deed of trust was canceled of record January 2, 1974.

Item Nineteen is a deed dated October 4, 1972, recorded in Book 581 on Page 155 Harnett County Registry. The deed was made by William A. Poole and wife Katie T. Poole, parties of the first part to First Baptist Church, party of the second part. The lot described therein is 140 ft. x 150 ft. located on the northwest corner of West Cumberland Street and South King Avenue. The property is known by members of the Church as the "Poole property" and is presently being used as the Church recreation area. Stocks in the approximate amount of $25,000.00 was given to the First Baptist Church by Mack M. Jernigan and Sallie N. Jernigan and designated by them for the express purpose of paying for this lot. At the conclusion of the morning worship service on Sunday, October 26, 1980 the congregation adjourned to this recreation area for the purpose of dedicating the area and naming it in honor of Mack M. Jernigan and Sallie N. Jernigan.

The Twentieth instrument is a deed dated August 30, 1975, made by Hannah H. Brannon, widow, party of the first part to First Baptist Church, party of the second part and recorded in Book 629 on Pages 771 and 772 Harnett County Registry. Part of the deed reads as follows: "in consideration of the sum of ten dollars and other good and valuable consideration----". For all practical purposes this was "a gift and charitable donation" by Mrs. Brannon to the Church. This is a lot fronting 25 feet on South Layton Avenue and running 150 feet "in a westerly direction along the line of the lot of the First Baptist Church of Dunn, and parallel with West Cumberland Street----". This increased the size of the parsonage lot from 75 ft. to 100 ft. on South Layton Avenue and made possible the construction of a parsonage driveway from South Layton Avenue and the closing the driveway from the very busy West Cumberland Street thoroughfare.

The Twenty-First and last transaction to date is a deed of trust dated July 28, 1978, and recorded in Book 675 on Page 666 Harnett County Registry, by First Baptist Church, Dunn, N. C., to Home Savings and Loan Association. of Dunn. The purpose of this loan in the amount of one hundred forty thousand and no/100 dollars to aid in the complete renovation of the Sunday school section first constructed in 1934. The real estate securing this note and deed of trust is the same as that appearing in Item One above. As of August 31, 1981, the note is in current condition and there remains a principal balance of $107,397.58.

In summary, there have been thirteen regular deeds, one quitclaim deed, one deed of subordination, one mortgage deed and five deeds of trusts, making a total of twenty-one transactions in all. The Church continues to retain title to lots described in Items 1, 8, 12, 19, 20 above.

Uses made of certain of the nine lots this Church has now or once had title to are referred to in the chapter on "Meeting Places" and the chapter on "Churches Formed By First Baptist Church".

20

Chapter III

Pastors of
First Baptist Church

No organization can continue to grow and be fruitful without constantly competent, energetic and dedicated leadership especially a missionary Baptist Church.

Each of the twenty pastors of this Church have been outstanding leaders and dedicated men. Visible evidence are such things as membership growth and stability, land acquisition and building programs, Churches formed, weaker Churches stabilized, etc.

More important, however, are the countless intangible and invisible evidences which have been so strongly felt by so many souls both within and without this congregation. Recorded below are their terms of office and a brief biographical sketch when available. The last three former pastors are still living and still active in Christian endeavors. May the pastors that follow be as dedicated and as strong leaders as all those who have gone before.

September 27, 1885 - Fall 1887

William Richard Johnson

Born - November 25, 1849 - Sampson County

Died - March 13, 1936 - Buried Cedar Creek Baptist Church Cemetery, Cumberland County

Organized, with the assistance of Rev. Wiley Page, this church and was its first pastor.

Pastor several other churches mostly of Cumberland and Sampson Counties.

Was present along with the second pastor, Rev. Isaac Thomas Newton, at the Fiftieth Anniversary Celebration of this church in 1935.

December 7, 1887 - September 2, 1888
Isaac Thomas Newton

Born - November 25, 1849, nine miles west of Fayetteville, N. C. on southern edge of present Ft. Bragg Reservation.

Died - December 7, 1944 while pastor of Piney Forest Baptist Church, buried in Piney Forest Church Cemetery, Columbus County, N. C.

Baptised - October 1875 by his Father Elder Reuben Newton

Licensed to preach August 28, 1882 by Rocky Mount Baptist Church on what is now Ft. Bragg Reservation and ordained by the same church on September 23, 1883.

Attended Donaldson Academy, Fayetteville, N. C.

Graduated Wake Forest College B.A. 1893

Married June 13, 1893 to Miss Hattie O Alderman who died May 27, 1894. Married December 29, 1896 to Miss Dixie Osborne of Brevard, N. C. who died June 28, 1947.

Five children: Mrs. A. C. (Anne Eliza) Talbott—

(Still living)

    Mr. Iri Thomas Newton—(Still living)
    Mrs. Barrington T. (Ruth Osborne) Hill—(Still living)
    Mrs. Hugh A. (Sarah Pauline) Moore—(Still living)
    Mrs. William R. (Josephine Caldwell) Fletcher—

(Still living)

Superintendent of Schools, Transylvania County N. C., 1903 -1904 and 1904-1905

Some of his Pastorates (on most occasions he served more
than one church at a time in "Fields")
Cedar Creek Baptist Association 1883-1885 and 1894-1895
    Rocky Mount 1883-1885
    Mt. Gilead 1894-1895
South River Baptist Association 1884-1888 and 1888-1891
    Spring Branch. 1884-1888
    Lilly's Grove 1884-1885
    Piney Grove 1886-1887
    Salem 1886-1887
    Royals Chapel 1886-1887
    Antioch 1887-1888
    Greenwood
    Dunn. 1887-1888
    Clement . . . . April-September 1888 and 1891-1892
Central Baptist Association 1890-1895
    New Hope (Wake County) 1890-1895
    Flat Rock 1891-1895
    Autryville. 1891-1892
Sandy Creek Baptist Association 1892-1893
    Carthage 1892-1893
    Cameron 1892-1893
    Cranes Creek 1892-1893
Raleigh Baptist Association 1893-1894
    Cameron 1893-1894
    Apex 1893-1894
    White Stone . . . . February-October 1894
Transylvania Baptist Association 1895-1904
    Brevard 1895-1903
    Rock Hill 1897-1905
    Mt. Moriah. 1895-1905
    Carson Creek
    Little River
    Zion
Broad River Baptist Association, South Carolina 1904-1906
    Buffalo
    Mt. Paran
    (Possibly two others)
Kings Mountain Baptist Association 1907-1912
    New Hope
    Fallston
    New Prospect
South Fork Baptist Association 1913-1917
    Dallas
    Long Creek
    Lowell
    Spencer Mountain

Cape Fear-Columbus-Columbus Baptist Association 1917-1944
Whiteville 1917-1925
Bolton
Fair Bluff
White Marsh 1919-1926
Chadbourn 1925-1934
Piney Forest 1930-1944
Lake Waccamaw 1933-1940
Oak Dale 1927-1929

Was instrumental in getting Dr. J. A. Campbell to accept pastorates at Spring Branch and Dunn when he resigned both these churches to enter Wake Forest College.

Member of the ordaining Presbytery when J. A. Campbell was ordained in November 1886 and offered the ordination prayer. Led the opening prayer at the funeral of Dr. Campbell on March 20, 1934.

One sentence from an editorial printed in The News Reporter, Whiteville, N. C. soon after the death of Rev. Newton is quoted below, "It was said that Rev. Newton influenced more people for good in Columbus County than any other person."

April 1, 1889 - November 9, 1890
Dr. James Archibald Campbell

Born - January 13, 1862 about ten miles from Campbell University on the road between Angier and Fuquay-Varina.

Died - March 18, 1934 - Buried in Buies Creek Cemetery March 20, 1934.

Baptised - October 27, 1872 by his father "Mr. Archie" into membership of Hector's Creek Baptist Church.

Ordained - November 1886 at Juniper Springs Baptist Church

Education: Attended Harnett Chapel (Suscription school) near his home at the age of six for a few months. Attended a grammar school at the age of ten with his father - Two months term. Attended boarding school in Apex at the age of seventeen. Attended Oak Dale Academy in Alamance County in 1881 for two years. Resigned as principal of "Union Academy" on January 13, 1885 to enter Wake Forest College. Remained at Wake Forest for Spring and Fall semesters of 1885 and Spring semester of 1886. Graduated Wake Forest College, 1911 B.A., 1926 D.D.

Teacher: Taught school first at age of seventeen for part of one year in the area of what is now Chalybeate Springs. A prepatory school was organized known as "Union Academy" at Winslow in northern Harnett County ten miles from Poe (now Buies Creek) with J. A. Campbell as headmaster. School opened on morning of January 7, 1884 with seventeen pupils and enrollment increased to seventy-eight before the first term was over. Resigned January 13, 1885 to enter Wake Forest College.

Organized "Buies Creek Academy" and classes began there January 5, 1887 with sixteen students. Headed this school, first as principal then as president, continously until his death on March 18, 1934.

Buies Creek Academy 1887-1926
Campbell Junior College 1926-1961
Campbell Senior College 1961-1979
Campbell University . . . . : June, 6, 1979-Present

Married - November 18, 1890 to Miss Cornelia Frances Pearson

Children: Leslie Hartwell Campbell, Arthur Carlyle Campbell and Mrs. A. E. (Elizabeth Pearson Campbell) Lynch.

Superintendent of Harnett County Schools 1890-1894 and 1897-1899

Pastorates:

Hectors's Creek . . . . October 1886 to--
Buies Creek Baptist Church . . . 1891-1895 and 1898-1934
Dunn Baptist Church 1889-1890
Spring Branch Baptist Church 1891-1931
Cannon Grove Baptist Church 1888
Holly Springs Baptist Church, Mt. Tabor Baptist Church, Averasboro Baptist Church, Benson Baptist Church, Coats Baptist Church, New Life Baptist Church, Green Level Baptist Church, Duke Baptist Church, Friendship Baptist Church and maybe others.

April 1, 1891 - December 29, 1892

Dr. William Frank Watson

Born September 5, 1862 - Fayetteville, N. C.

Died July 16, 1920 Alexander, Virginia - Buried Gastonia, N.C.

Ordained 1886 at Wake Forest Baptist Church

Graduated Wake Forest College B.A. 1886

Honorary D. D. University of Richmond 1912

Pastor First Baptist Church, Gastonia, N. C. 1899 - 1903

Other Pastorates:

First Baptist Church, Edenton, N. C.

First Baptist Church, Monroe, N. C.

Spurgeon's Memorial Baptist Church, Norfolk, Virginia

South Street Baptist Church, Portsmouth, Virginia

First Baptist Church, Alexandria, Virginia, August 1, 1908 - January 5, 1916

March 2, 1893 - April 15, 1894
Dr. Needham Bryan Cobb

Born February 1, 1836 - Jones County, N. C.

Died May 31, 1905 - Sampson County, N. C.

Education: University of North Carolina - B. A. & M. A., Judson College, Marion, Alabama - D. D. 1889. Principal, Lilesville Academy when Wilson B. Morton was student. Licensed attorney-at-law and practiced in Pitt, Wayne and Green Counties.

Vestryman in Episcopal Church until Oct. 1859

Baptised into Greenville Baptist Church

Ordained in Wilson Baptist Church 1860

Commissioned as Chaplain in Confederate Army June 12, 1861, and served three years

President N. C. Baptist State Convention 1879, 1880 and 1881

Retired to his farm in Sampson County, N. C. 1895

November 1, 1894 - June 9, 1895
Dr. William Cary Newton

Born October 6, 1873 - Kerr, Sampson Co., N. C.

Died December 24, 1966 - Richmond, Va.

Wake Forest College - B. A. 1895; D. D. 1925

Rochester Theological Seminary - Th.G. 1898

Ordained Wake Forest 1893

Missionary to Nigeria 1889 for one year

Appointed Missionary to China October 6, 1902, and remained a Missionary to China for 37 years

January 12, 1896 - June 15, 1896
J. G. Pulliam

Born August 27, 1857, McDowell County, N. C.
Student at Judson College, N. C.
Southern Baptist Theological Seminary 1885 - 1886
Ordained Coweta Baptist Church, Franklin, N. C. March 1886
Pastor Franklin, N. C. February 1886 - January 1887
Pastor LaConner, Washington March 1887 - September 1889 .
Elected President of Northwest Baptist Association, Washington June 15, 1889
Appointed State Missionary of Montana, November 26, 1889
Gen. My. A.B.H.M. Society for Montana
Pastor in Northern Idaho 1890 - 1891
Pastor in Woodland, California 1892 - 1894
Pastor Baptist Church, Smithfield, N. C. 1895
Pastor Dunn Baptist Church, Dunn, N. C. January 12, 1896 - June 15, 1896
Pastor Granite Falls Baptist Church, Granite Falls, N. C. 1897
Living first in Plano, Texas and then in Wellington, Texas 1904 - 1907
Pastor Big Stone Gap Baptist Church, Big Stone Gap, Virginia 1908 - 1909

June 24, 1896 - August 1, 1900
Luther Rice Carroll

Born December 23, 1838, near Magnolia, N. C.

Died November 13, 1905 - Buried Old Town Cemetery, Warsaw, N. C.

Attended public schools and academies in Duplin County, N. C.

Confederate Army - April 15, 1861 - April, 1865

Married January 27, 1867, to Miss Jemima Ann Carlton - no children

School teacher, farmer and Baptist Minister

Ordained December 13, 1896, Warsaw Baptist Church, Warsaw, N. C. at age of 58

Pastorates: Dunn, Mt. Olive, Island Creek, Faison and Poplar Grove, all in North Carolina

Tallest of all pastors of First Baptist Church — 6' 7''.

January 1, 1901 - October 1, 1902
William Charles Barrett

Born February 27, 1869 - Moore County, N. C.

Died June 29, 1930 - Laurinburg, N. C.

Wake Forest College B. A. 1896

Southern Baptist Theological Seminary

Other Pastorates: Durham, N. C., First Baptist Church, Gastonia, N. C. November 1, 1911 - December 31, 1927

Wife: Miss Ruby McKay, Laurinburg, N. C. Children: Margaret, Charles, Ruby, John

Resigned from Gastonia, N. C. church for health reasons.

April 1, 1903 - January 1, 1904
Dr. Wilson Bunyan Morton

Born February 19, 1856 - Lilesville, N. C.

Died March 12, 1925. Buried Oaklawn Cemetery, Louisburg, N. C.

Ordained June 8, 1884

Education: Lilesville Academy, Wake Forest College LL.B-1884 and Southern Baptist Theological Seminary

During his career he became a very successful optometrist in Louisburg, North Carolina

Other Pastorates: Weldon, Sharon, Gardner's, Littleton, Louisburg, Roxboro, Marion, Columbia, New Bethel, White Level, all in North Carolina

Married to Miss Annie Upperman, Louisburg, N. C. Two Children: Wilson B. Morton, Jr. and Elizabeth Morton

United States Commissioner

November, 1905 - December 31, 1911

Dr. Willis Richard Cullom

Born January 15, 1867 - Halifax County, N. C.

Died October 20, 1963 - Wake Forest, N. C.

Education: Wake Forest College M. A. 1892, Southern Baptist Theological Seminary Th.M. 1895; Th.D. 1904 and University of Richmond D. D. 1915

In 1896, the trustees of Wake Forest College invited him "to inaugurate the study of Bible" as part of the curriculum. Taught Bible for 42 years at Wake Forest College.

Served as interim pastor several times at First Baptist Church, Dunn, North Carolina including the two years seven months when this church was without a pastor.

February 1, 1912 - November, 1914

James Long

Born Union County, North Carolina

Died December 28, 1939

Ordained February 18, 1892, Warrenton, N. C.

Education: Yadkin Mineral Springs Institute, Wake Forest College B. A. 1892 and Rochester Theological Seminary T. S. 1895

Some other Pastorates: Phelps, N. Y., First Baptist Church, Laurinburg, N. C. from February 1915 to 1919.

July 1, 1917 - January 27, 1918

Dr. John Alston [Jack] Ellis

Born - January 29, 1882 Harpers Cross Roads, Chatham County, N. C.

Died - July 4, 1960 Restlawn Memorial Gardens, Raleigh, N.C. (Raleigh-Durham Highway)

Baptised - Cool Springs Baptist Church, Sanford, N. C. August 25, 1889

Ordained - Forestville, N. C. 1909

Wake Forest College B. A. 1911, M. A. 1912, D. D. 1928

Southern Baptist Theological Seminary B. D., Th. M., Th. D.

Army Chaplain W. W. 1 January 1918 - July 1919

Some Pastorates: First Baptist Church, Dunn, N. C. July 1, 1917 - January 27, 1918. Pullen Memorial Baptist Church, Raleigh September 7, 1919 to January 13, 1929. First Baptist Church, Sherman, Texas 1929 to April 1951 (Retired).

Interim Pastorates after first retirement: First to Roanoke, Virginia, then to Parkwood Baptist Church, Portsmouth, Virginia, then to Tabernacle Baptist Church, Raleigh, N. C. After a few months as pastor at Tabernacle he was called as full time regular pastor, Sept. 1951 and retired the second time sometime in 1956 following an auto accident in January 1956 which impaired his health from which he never fully recovered.

Married October 21, 1919 to Miss Helen Mary Becker, Roanoke, Virginia (Still Living)

Four Children: Mrs. William A. (Elaine) Bond, John Alston Ellis, Jr., Mrs. John P. (Mary Gordon) Livingston, Jr. and Leland Caswell Ellis

Member of Executive Committee of Texas Baptist General Convention for many years.

Twice elected Chairman of Board of Directors of the Biblical Recorder in the 1950's.

June 2, 1918 - June, 1921

Eugene Irving Olive

Born December 7, 1890 - Wake County, N. C.

Died March 6, 1968 - Winston-Salem, N. C.

Education: Buies Creek Academy, Wake Forest College B. A. 1910 and Southern Baptist Theological Seminary Th.M. 1918

Pastor Wake Forest Baptist Church and College Chaplain

Wake Forest Alumni Director and many other responsibilities on College staff

Acting Editor of Biblical Recorder November 1941 to November 1942

Came to First Baptist Church of Dunn as bachelor pastor.

Found his future wife, Miss Iva Pearson in choir loft directing the choir. Married in Raleigh June 29, 1926.

November, 1921 - January 1, 1929

Elbert Neil Johnson

Born February 3, 1886 - Sampson County

Died February 26, 1969 - Buried Spring Hill Cemetery, Wagram, N. C.

Education: Del School, Delway, N. C., Wake Forest College B. A. 1910 and Southern Baptist Theological Seminary Th.M. 1912

Pastorates: Morganton, Reidsville, Dunn, Mount Olive, Fair Bluff, Bear Swamp, Wagram, All in North Carolina

Married to Miss Frances Livingston Johnson, Raleigh, N. C., Daughter of Livingston and Fannie Memory Johnson (One time editor of Biblical Recorder)

Children: Dr. Meredith Johnson, Mrs. Elizabeth J. Hudson and Dr. Elbert Neil Johnson, Jr.

Wrote a book published in 1955 entitled "THE MASTER IS HERE"

In his later years, he wrote a number of hymns (Probably 130 hymns and poems) the first of which was chosen as the "Centennial Hymn" for the Southern Baptist Theological Seminary, and he was present when it was sung by the entire Southern Baptist Convention. Two others of his hymns were published by the American Hymn Society. One, "The Silver Trumpet", and anthem for men's voices and brass quintet, was first performed by the Alabama Singing Men at the Southern Baptist Convention in 1980, and was used by that group in its tour that year. Probably only three of his hymns have been published at this time. However, his great-nephew, Nathan Corbett, a music missionary in Africa at the present time, has the right to set his hymns to music and probably other of his hymns will be published.

April 15, 1929 - April 15, 1939

Dr. Eugene Norfleet Gardner

Born November 12, 1894 - Franklin, Virginia

Died May 12, 1968 - Buried City Cemetery, Franklin, Virginia

Education: University of Richmond B. A. 1914, M. A. 1915, D. D. 1952, University of Chicago B. D., Southern Baptist Theological Seminary Th. M.

Baptised 1907, Franklin Baptist Church, Franklin, Virginia

Ordained at Franklin, Virginia October 15, 1915 (Franklin Baptist Church)

Pastorates include: Sycamore Baptist Church, Franklin, Virginia, Buckhorn Baptist Church, Como, N. C., Robert's Chapel Baptist Church, Pendleton, N. C., Orphanage Pastor (Thomasville, N. C.), First Baptist Church, Dunn.

N. C., First Baptist Church, Henderson, N. C., First Baptist Church, Laurinburg, N. C. (Retired and moved back to Henderson, N. C.)

Professor Bible - Orphanage High School, Thomasville, N. C. 1925-1929

Professor of Bible - Campbell College - Six Years (While Pastor at Dunn, N. C.)

Trustee of Wingate College

State President of Baptist Training Union

President of General Board (Two Years) N. C. State Convention

Acting editor of "Charity & Children

Member of Board of Directors, Biblical Recorder

Member of Board of Directors of North Carolina Conference for Social Services

President of Three Rotary Clubs (Dunn, Henderson, Laurinburg)

Member of the Relief & Annuity Board, the Hospital Commission and the Foreign Mission Board (All Southern Baptist Convention)

Recording Secretary of the Baptist State Convention of North Carolina for Eight Years (Serving at time of his death) and several other responsible positions with the Convention.

Author of many books including: "Old Testament Characters", "Lamp Unto My Feet", "Magnifying The Church", "Journey To Japan", "Always The Ten Commandments", "Changing Patterns In Christian Programs", "Ruth"

Married (First) to Miss Ruth Carver December 30, 1920 (Daughter of Dr. & Mrs. W. O. Carver). To this union two daughters: Mrs. Robert (Lelia Norfleet) Hathoway, Richmond, Virginia and Mrs. J. L. (Alice Ruth) Wilson, Winston-Salem, N. C.

Married (Second) to Mrs. Mattie Macon White July 16, 1944 (Widow of a Foreign Missionary)

November 1, 1939 - September 15, 1942

Dr. Thomas W. Fryer

Born January 14, 1905 - Chadbourn, North Carolina

Still Living (retired) Ocoee, Florida

Education: Southern Baptist Theological Seminary Th.M.

Roanoke College, Salem, Va., D. D.

Pastorates: Clintwood, Va., Scottsboro, Va., Martinsville, Va., Danville, Va., Suffolk, Va., First Baptist Church, Dunn, North Carolina, Second Baptist Church, New Bern, North Carolina, Stuanton Memorial Baptist Church, Miami, Fla., College Park Baptist Church, Florence, South Carolina

Married to the former Miss Pauline Harp, of Galax, Va.

Three Children: Dr. Thomas W. Fryer, Jr., Mountain View, Cal., Mrs. Richard Compton, Johnson City, Tenn. and Mrs. Milton Skipper, Marion, S. C.

December 1, 1942 - June 1, 1949
S. Lewis Morgan, Jr.

Born August 3, 1911

Still living in Washington, D. C.

Education: Wake Forest College A. B. 1932, Duke University School of Religion 1936 and Southeastern Baptist Theological Seminary Th. M. 1938

Pastorates: Clinton Baptist Church, Clinton, N. C. 1938-1942 First Baptist Church, Dunn, N. C. 1942-1949, Petworth-Montgomery Baptist Church, Washington, D. C. 1949-1968, Washington Pastorial Counseling Service, Washington, D. C. 1968----present

Married to the former Miss Cynthia Siler in 1938

Two Children: Lewis Marshall Morgan and Mrs. Roger (Cynthia Mahan) Diggle

Presently married to the former Ina Grim

Executive Committee North Carolina Baptist State Convention 1948, Southern Baptist Hospital Board 1951, Foreign Mission Board, Southern Baptist Convention 1956-1962

Listed in Who's Who in Religion 1975ff.

August 1, 1949 - July 31, 1961

Ernest Parker Russell

Born June 30, 1911 - Stanley County, N. C.

Still living - retired in Albemarle, N. C.

Education: West End High School, West End, N. C., Draughon's Business College, Winston-Salem, N. C., Wake Forest College B.A. 1944, Southern Baptist Theological Seminary 1947 Th.M., "Who's Who in American Colleges and Universities", Bookkeeper and Office Manager - Armour & Co. 1930-1941

Pastorates: Corenth Baptist Church, Louisburg, N. C. 1942-1944, Inez Baptist Church, Inez, N. C. - 1942-1944, Brown's Baptist Church, Warrenton, N. C. - 1944, New Castle Baptist Church, New Castle, Ky. - 1944-1947, Green Sea Baptist Church, Green Sea, S. C. - 1947-1949, First Baptist Church, Dunn, N. C. - 1949-1961, McGill Street Baptist Church, Concord, N. C. - 1961-1972 and Dunn's Mountain Baptist Church, Salisbury, N. C. - 1972-1975

Trustee Campbell University

Trustee Meredith College

Member of "Committee of 100" Campbell University

N. C. Baptist State Convention Committee on "Advance Program of our Colleges"

Member General Board Kentucky General Association

Married to the former Dorothy Dowd Crutchfield and they have two daughters, Mrs. Charles A. (Elizabeth Dowd) Wilson and Mrs. David K. (Mary Ann) Lawson

45

April 15, 1962 - Present

Dr. Thomas Moten Freeman

Wake Forest University B. A. 1939

Southern Baptist Theological Seminary Th.M. 1942

Campbell University D. D. 1972

Pastorates: Rural Churches, Johnston County, North Carolina, Hocutt Memorial Baptist Church, Burlington, N. C., Middle River Baptist Church, Baltimore, Md. and First Baptist Church, Dunn, N. C.

Member General Board, N. C. Baptist State Convention

Member Board of Directors, Biblical Recorder

Trustee of Wake Forest University

Trustee of Campbell University

Member of Executive Committee Southern Baptist Convention

First Vice-President, N. C. Baptist State Convention 1970-1971 and 1971-1972

President, N. C. Baptist State Convention 1972-1973 and 1973-1974

President, N. C. Christian Action League

Chairman, Governor's Good Neighbor Council, Dunn and Harnett County, North Carolina

Married July 24, 1942 to Miss Maisie Castlebury, Apex, N. C.

Children: Dr. William Hardin Freeman, Mrs. Jan (Ann Sinclair) Gazenbeek, Mrs. Edward (Judith Louise) McRae and Mrs. Kenneth (Joy Ruth) Tilley

Chapter IV

Meeting Places
and Building Programs

Meeting places of any organization hold many values both from a sentimental and a historical point of view, not only for its own membership but for the general public. For this reason along with others it is fitting that records and historical sketches should devote a part to this important matter.

On September 27, 1885, the "Greenwood Baptist Church" was organized in the Greenwood School House, formerly the Pope School House. Where was the Greenwood School House and was the school a public or private school? On June 25, 1888, two people on this same day died in the newly incorporated Town of Dunn, N. C. One was William F. Jones, Age 32, son of D. and M. M. Jones and the other was Ralph Jerome Jones, Age 14 months, son of D. A. and V. A. Jones.

The Town of Dunn had not provided for a municipal cemetery. Therefore, the City Commissioners met in an emergency session and appointed three men to select a suitable municipal burial site. They made their selection approximately one mile from the town limits at that time near the Greenwood School House site. The land was owned by Henry Pope and wife, Eliza Pope.

Mr. & Mrs. Pope evidentally gave their consent for the interment of these two. At the proper time the two were buried side by side in graves due east and west.

The committee appointed by the Town Commissioners and Mr. & Mrs. Henry Pope evidentally had another agreement since in the Registry of Harnett County there is recorded a deed in Book B-2 on Page 12, dated September 14, 1888. The deed was executed by Henry Pope and wife, Eliza Pope, parties of the first part, to S. W. Parker, Dr. M. W. Harper, J. T. Phillips, J. J. Wade and A. T. Massingill, Commissioners of the Town of Dunn, parties of the second part. A section of this deed reads as follows: "that said parties of the first part in consideration of Fifty Dollars ($50.00) Dollars, to them paid by the said parties of the second part, the receipt of which is hereby acknowledged, have bargained and sold and by these presents do bargain sell and convey to said parties of the second part and their successors in office a certain tract or parcel of land near Dunn, Harnett County, State of North Carolina, adjoining the lands of Henry Pope, for the use of a cemetery for the Town of Dunn: Bounded as follows: Beginning at a stake and runs north 71-12/100 yards to a stake then west 71-12/100 yards to a stake then south 71-12/100 yards to a stake then east 71-12/00 yards to the beginning, containing five thousand and fifty-eight square yards (5058) or one acre and a circle in the center of said lot fifty feet in diameter.''

It has been said and there is very good reason to believe that this circle was first placed there to designate the location of Pope's Schoolhouse which name was later changed to Greenwood Schoolhouse. The circle is still there today, still fifty feet in diameter, in the center of the intersection of two streets and forming a circular drive around a gazebo in the center of the circle. This spot also continues to mark the center of the original Greenwood Cemetery. The two original graves mentioned above are eighty-five feet due east from the center of the circle.

There is another infant grave on this same plot with the two original graves and is located at the foot of the infant Ralph Jerome Jones (one of the two original graves). The inscription on the headstone of this grave reads: "Carl Waveland Jones, son of D. A. and V. A. Jones, died July 12, 1884, age 10 months''. The way this grave is crowded into the plat, the position of both the headstone and footstone as they relate to the other stones and the relationship of the two infants graves is compelling evidence that the body of Carl Waveland Jones was first interred at some other place and was, at a later date, re-interred at this place...perhaps after the death of his father which occurred March 6, 1891, and whose body is also buried on this plot.

Mr. Henry Pope deeded the property to the Town of Dunn in such a way that it lies due east and west between north and south which is the way most cemeteries have been laid out for thousands of years. However, the streets of the original town of Dunn are laid out perpendicular to the railroad and the avenues and alleys run parallel to the railroad. Since the railroad does not run due north and south through Dunn, the town is off true north and south or true east and west by several degrees. This accounts for the fact that South Orange Avenue comes into Greenwood Cemetery at an angle rather than perpendicular.

A careful search of the records in the offices of the Harnett County Board of Education between the years 1882 and 1888 reveals no mention of a Pope's School or a Greenwood School. The land on which this schoolhouse was located belonged to Henry Pope. It is reasonable, therefore, to assume that Greenwood School was a private school rather than a Harnett County operated school.

So much about the location of the Greenwood Schoolhouse and some history about the cemetery. After some discussion the Greenwood Baptist Church decided to move from the schoolhouse into the Town of Dunn and made such a move in the spring of 1887. As a result the official name of the Church was changed from "Greenwood Baptist Church" to "Dunn Baptist Church". The first meeting place in the Town of Dunn was over the buggy repair shop owned by Allen B. Godwin. Later this building was torn down and a dwelling house built there. In 1931, Mr. and Mrs. Jacob A. Underwood were living in this dwelling. A review of the early Dunn City Directories reveals that the address of Mr. & Mrs. Underwood at that time was 211 South Railroad Avenue. This would cause the dwelling to face the railroad and be on the northeast corner of East Divine Street and South Railroad Avenue adjoining the Bowen law office building and at present is a vacant lot. On June 1, 1887, the Church purchased a lot (Item One, Chapter Two) and immediately began the construction of a wooden Church. The building program of this Church house began under the capable leadership of their first pastor, W. R. Johnson, and was completed under the very fine and dedicated leadership of their second pastor, I. Tommie Newton.

The stay above the buggy repair shop was short lived and the congregation moved to the second floor of the James Addison Taylor Store located on Britt Alley. There was a private school on this same floor during week days and the purpose of this move was to be able to take advantage of the School's furniture and equipment. The Church remained here until it moved into its new wooden Church in May, 1888.

In the early days of Dunn, many prominent businesses were fronting on alleys as well as streets and avenues. For instance, a Mr. Hodges in the latter part of 1902 rented the first floor of a building on Lucknow Alley and established a business there known as Catfish Lumber Company. That portion of Britt Alley concerned here runs from West Broad Street to West Cumberland Street between what is now Home Federal Savings and Loan Association and Skinner and Drew Funeral Home. The Taylor Store building faced the east side of Britt Alley. The wooden Church was dedicated, including a note burning ceremony, on May 29, 1892, while the fourth pastor, W. Frank Watson, served the Church. The dedicatory sermon was preached by Rev. C. Durham.

50

The wooden Church continued to be the meeting place from May, 1888, until December, 1914. Membership growth was consistant. The Sunday School was very active. Between 1906 and 1911, under the leadership of their eleventh pastor, Dr. W. R. Cullom, four Sunday School classrooms were added for the growing Sunday School.

It soon became evident, however, that continuing to add to the wooden Church for its growing needs was impractical if not impossible and so interest began to stimulate toward the construction of a new brick Church. In the fall of 1912, Mr. J. M. McMichael was secured as the architect who developed plans in the style of the Romansque order of architeture, having elegant stained glass windows and being surmounted by a majestic dome covered with copper. A Mr. Cooper was employed as contractor and construction began in early 1913. The planning, development and construction was under the capable, dedicated and devoted leadership of the Church's twelfth pastor, the Rev. James Long.

The auditorium and several classrooms of this brick Church was occupied in December, 1914. This same building, plus two additions continues to be in the Church building of the First Baptist Church of Dunn today. Dedication services and note burning ceremonies of this new Church was held Sunday morning, April 2, 1922, under the leadership of its pastor at that time (fifteenth pastor) Rev. Elbert N. Johnson. A very detailed account of this service can be found in the April 4, 1922, issue of the Dunn Dispatch, Volume 8, No. 104. Excerpts from this news article are quoted below:

"An excellent and interesting program had been planned. The Chairman of the Building Committee, Mr. J. C. Clifford, read many congratulatory messages, letters and telegrams from former pastors and friends. A very fitting word of felicitation was sent by the First Presbyterian Church of Dunn. Dr. Livingston Johnson, Editor of the Biblical Recorder, Raleigh, N. C., spoke briefly in behalf of the 300,000 white Baptists of North Carolina."

"The sermon was perhaps the most impressive feature of the service. Dr. W. J. McGlothlin, the President of Furman University, Greenville, S. C., delivered the dedicatory sermon. Few men in all America can present the Gospel with greater clarity and power than this unusual preacher. He chose as his subject "The significance of the Church Building'. The text of Scripture used is in I Tim. 3:15 'The

House of God, which is the Church of the Living God, The Pillar and Ground of the Truth'.''

Immediately following the sermon, Mr. J. C. Clifford came forward and burned the last of the notes and mortgages in the presence of the congregation. As the fire was burning the last vestage of indebtedness on the Church, he spoke most feelingly as follows: 'now as these the only visible evidence of our indebtedness turn to ashes, we blot from our memory the labor, hardship, self-denial, and privations endured to make possible this day, and remember alone the pleasure which has come to us in being accorded the joyous privilege of making a few sacrifices for Him'.''

''Following that was the dedicatory prayer offered by Rev. J. A. Campbell, former pastor, and greatly beloved in Harnett County. It was a precious and Holy moment as the Church gave their beautiful Temple to their God.''

In the early 1930's the Church began to realize once. again that its Sunday School had grown so large and become so active that the enlargement of physical facilities was an absolute necessity if the Sunday School was to continue to expand. These were the depression years and it took a lot of grit, determination and faith to even seriously think of and certainly to begin another building program.

Dr. E. Norfleet Gardner was pastor at this time (sixteenth) and under his superb leadership, definite plans developed and a major undertaking got underway. Part of the October, 1934, Church Bulletin dated October 7, 1934, reads as follows: ''At an enthusiastic Church conference last Wednesday blueprints for a proposed Church annex, to be used as an educational building, were presented and adopted. The sentiment of the people was to put up a structure that would accommodate the crowds that overrun the present Sunday School, and make it possible to reach out for hundreds not enlisted in the teaching of the Church.''

"The building committee for the annex is composed of: Geo. T. Noel, M. M. Jernigan, George F. Pope, Dr. C. D. Bain, W. P. Dickey, Mrs. C. D. Bain, J. C. Jones, Herbert B. Taylor, J. P. Morgan, and W. L. Aldredge.''

The November, 1934, bulletin dated November 11, 1934, also reads in part as follows: ''were you present for the breaking of the grounds for the educational building of our Church Friday afternoon? We shall follow each week the progress made in the erection of this building to the glory of God and the training of our citizens in His word. Our Sunday School Superintendent, Mack M. Jernigan, deserves much credit for the initiation of this movement. George T. Neol is Chairman of the Building Committee; and Herbert B. Taylor of the Finance Committee. Under the leadership of these men we shall move forward unitedly towards the construction of a beautiful and efficient place in which to teach and direct the life of our growing Church.''

This Church annex is the three story sturcture connected to the east side of the original brick Church and extends to the alley, officially known as ''Church Alley'' and is the same structure that was completely renovated in 1978. But that's another story. Let's continue on with this one.

In the December, 1934, Church Bulletin dated December 8, 1934, there is the following: ''We rejoice in the progress made in the annex these last weeks. On 'Thanksgiving Day' (November 22, 1934) after we had observed the custom of worship at the sunrise hour, we laid the cornerstone given by Mr. and Mrs. R. A. Duncan. Today the walls are far advanced on the second story of the building.''

''At the laying of the cornerstone the following articles were placed within and sealed: a copy of the New Testament, put there by the Superintendent of the Bible School, M. M. Jernigan; copies of the ''Charity and Children'', ''Biblical Recorder'', ''Home and Foreign Fields'' and the W.M.U. Year Book of the First Baptist Church; copies of the ''Dunn Dispatch'', ''Daily Bulletin'' and ''Dunn Scout Booster''; Church monthly bulletins for January and November, 1934; Sunday School record for last Sunday; copy of some of the correspondence from Dr. Charles E. Maddry, Executive Secretary of the Foreign Mission Board, to the pastor relative to his becoming Superintendent of the Italian-Spanish Mission of Southern Baptists, photographs of a class of intermediate girls with their teacher, Mrs. C. L. Guy, and of the pastor.''

A new boiler for the Church heating plant was purchased of sufficient size to heat both the original Church and the new annex at a cost of $575.17 but was not to be delivered until Friday, January 18, 1935. Because of no heat the morning Church services for January 20, 1935, were held in the high school building and the night services were called off. The high school building at that time was where it is at the present time in the 400 block of North Orange Avenue and on the west side of said avenue.

The February 1937 Church Bulletin dated February 7, 1937, has additional information about the new annex, part of which so reads: "This Sunday the lower floor has been opened up for the use of the cradle roll, beginners and primary departments. How happy we are over this accomplishment. Later we shall continue with certain needed interior finishings but already we are able to use the entire building."

We read in the Church Conference Minutes of March 17, 1937, that Mrs. C. L. Guy issued an invitation to attend her Sunday School class house warming in the educational building on March 19, 1937, at 7:30 p.m. Therefore, by February, 1937, use of the entire new annex building was a reality and there was great joy in the hearts of all the Church family.

Under the dedicated leadership, council and guidance of the nineteenth pastor. Rev. Ernest P. Russell, the Church membership began to realize again that the Church would need in the not too distant future to provide additional much needed building space for the continued healthy and rapid growth of its Sunday School. Accordingly, the Church purchased a lot 140 ft. x 150 ft., known as the "Hood property" for use as a future building site for an additional educational annex. For a more complete description of this property reference is made to Item Twelve, Chapter II, of this work.

At the time of purchase there was on this lot a spacious two-story dwelling in rather poor condition which was the former home of the "Hood family". Until in the future when this building needed to be dismantled for the purpose of erecting the additional annex, it was decided to temporarily occupy this dwelling with part of the Sunday School. After some very preliminary renovations, departments one and two were moved into this dwelling on August 5, 1956.

In the summer of 1962 the First Presbyterian Church of Dunn moved into their beautiful new building at 901 North Park Avenue and that left vacant their old building on the corner of West Cumberland Street and South Layton Avenue. The First Presbyterian Church, over the years, has always been most cooperative with the First Baptist Church, and so in a regular conference of the First Baptist Church on October 18, 1962, there is found in the minutes of that meeting the following: "Earl Jones was recognized and advised that he had consulted with the Presbyterian authorities and that the old educational plant was available to our Church for the cost of paying the insurance and the utilities. The Presbyterians will want written agreement if we accept their offer. Motion by Max McLeod seconded by L. L. Coats that we begin using this facility at the earliest possible date. Motion carried."

Following this action we find in the Church Builder of October 30, 1962, an announcement that Adult Departments I & II will meet on Sunday November 4, 1962, in the Old Presbyterian Church building and that beginning Sunday November 11, 1962, these departments will have both their assemblies and classes in these quarters. Counting back, we find that these two departments met in the Hood building for six years and approximately three months.

Now that the Hood building had become vacant we find in the minutes of the regular Church conference on February 14, 1963, the following motion: "that the Church trustees sell, for the Church, the Hood building to Willard Mixon T/A Pope and Mixon, for the sum of $375.00 cash. That Mr. Mixon is to remove the building by June 1, 1963 -- that if he fails to have it moved by this date he is to forfeit any part of the building which remains on the Church lot. Motion carried."

Dr. Thomas Moten Freeman accepted the pastorate of this Church effective April 15, 1962. Since that time, under his dedicated and highly skilled leadership and with the enthusiastic following of the Congregation, one new building has been constructed and three very major renovations of existing buildings have been completed and another renovation program is in progress.

In the Church Builder dated October 8, 1963, there is this statement "Last Sunday (October 6, 1963) we made a decision to build an educational unit on the Hood lot." In the Church builder of April 14, 1964, this statement appears: "Our Church adopts plans for the new building last Sunday." (April 12, 1964)

In the Builder of May 12, 1964, this appears: "In a called meeting last Sunday (May 10, 1964) our Church voted to adopt the program presented by the Building Finance Committee. It involves the effort to raise $200,000.00 during the next five years or $40,000.00 a year. The membership will be canvassed by May 31st and everyone will be asked to make a pledge. We have prayed and planned, now we must add our contributions in cash."

On July 14, 1964, the Building Committee said: "We are proposing that we give priority to the adult classrooms that will be built under the auditorium and that we try to get them completed in time to move our adults from the annex into the new rooms by October 1st." About July 21, 1964, in reference to the lower auditorium, the building committee upon the advice of the architect, John James Croft, Jr., recommended that the Church employ Keith Finch, of Merit Construction Company, to do this work on a time and materials basis. This project is estimated to cost $40,000.00. On Sunday, July 26, 1964, the Church in conference adopted this recommendation and soon construction began. This project was completed the latter part of November, 1964, and a statement in the Church Builder dated December 1, 1964, says: "WE'RE IN AT LAST!" We have moved from the old Presbyterian building into the renovated basement of our auditorium." Departments I & II of our Sunday School were at last back home in permanent quarters after eight years and approximately four months.

On Sunday, August 30, 1964, after the morning worship service the Church was called into conference and by unanimous vote authorized the building committee to enter a contract with the D. R. Allen & Son Construction Company to erect the new educational building on the Hood lot. The contract price was $135,500.00. Construction began about two weeks later and continued at a normal rate.

In the Church Builder of June 22, 1965, there is this statement: "THE BEGINNING OF A NEW ERA!" The cutting of the ribbon last Sunday morning (June 20, 1965) and the opening of our new educational building marked the beginning of a new era. This is the first new building for our Bible teaching program since 1934." In the Church conference on August 11, 1965, the minutes record that Mr. S. D. Whittington, Chairman of the Building Committee, advised that the new educational building had been turned over and accepted by the Church as of August 11, 1965. Another building program had been brought to a successful conclusion.

In 1967, another big renovation project was begun. On Sunday, August 27, 1967, the Church by unanimous vote decided to renovate the Sancturay. This would consist of:

(1) having the pews removed, repaired, refinished and reinstalled
(2) having the Sanctuary repainted
(3) have new carpet installed in the Sanctuary, choir, vestibule, and entrances to the auditorium

Request was also made to study the Sanctuary lighting system. The Church was informed at this time that the pews were scheduled to be removed on Monday, September 4, and that they would be out for about thirty days.

The following Sunday, September 3, 1967, discussion was entered into as to whether, during renovation, worship services should be held in the high school auditorium or to use the Church lower auditorium. To use the lower auditorium would require two identical services...one at 8:30 a.m. and one at 11:00 a.m., because the congregation could not all be seated at once. Pastor Tom Freeman agreed to conduct the two services and the Church voted to use the lower auditorium in preference to the high school. At this same conference it accepted an offer of $1,000.00 to replace the auditorium lights.

In the Church Builder for October 10, 1967, it was announced that the carpet supplier was behind schedule and that the next scheduled delivery date was November 1, 1967. This, of course, delayed delivery of the pews and prolonged the necessity for having two worship services each Sunday.

On Tuesday, November 21, 1967, it was announced that: "Our annual Thanksgiving service is planned for 7:00 a.m. on Thursday morning in the Church Sanctuary. The Fairview Church Furniture Co. will try to have the pews in the main floor for our use then." Thus the Sanctuary was used on November 23, 1967, for the first time since September 3, 1967. This projects actual cost was $12,191.16, plus the lights for which $2,000.00 was contributed."

About ten years passed before another (the biggest) renovation project began. For more than twenty years serious consideration had been given to completely renovate the educational plant which was built in 1934. An architect was employed and his floor plans for renovation of the old education unit was distributed to each Church family, beginning Sunday, July 10, 1977, for their study and consideration and these plans were approved by the Church on August 14, 1977.

On December 4, 1977, the Church voted to enter into a remodeling program of the old education unit which was expected to take from seven to nine months. Keith Finch T/A Merit Construction Co., was employed on a time and material basis and work began during this month of December. This project consisted of removing the entire inside of the building, leaving only the outside walls and the roof, and completely rebuild the entire three floors. It also included reworking the two classrooms behind the choir to include a secretary's office plus work room, a pastor's study and a conference room.

Work proceeded with dispatch and with excellent skill and attention to detail. On October 4, 1978, it was announced that October 15 would be "Occupation Day" for this renovated beautiful building and it actually occurred on that date. Once more another building program had been brought to a successful conclusion. The total cost was $274,202.18.

On Sunday, November 26, 1978, after the morning worship service the congregation gathered outside the Church to witness the removal of the cornerstone laid on Thanksgiving morning, November 22, 1934, a period of 16,075 days. Contents of the stone as previously listed in this chapter were observed. The following Sunday December 3, 1978, the congregation again gathered outside the Church after the morning worship service to witness the ceremony of laying the new cornerstone. All the artifacts that came out of the 1934 stone plus the new materials listed below were placed in a corner box, sealed airtight and watertight, and placed in the new stone:

> A Good News New Testament
> The Biblical Recorder Paper
> Charity and Children Paper
> The Dunn Daily Record
> The Pastor's Sermon for that day
> The Thanksgiving Program, November 23, 1978
> Two Sunday Worship Programs
> Directory of Church Officers
> Directory of Sunday School Workers
> Names of Resident Church Members
> Copies of First Baptist Builder
> Visitation Folder
> Visitor Welcome Card
> Copy of 75th Anniversary Program
> Copy of Church Budget
> Copy of Financial Report for October, 1978

A Church Yearbook for 1940
Copies of Sunday School Paper
List of Building Planning Committee
Convention and Dorcas Sunday School Class Rolls
Beginner Certificate for 1912
Promotion Certificate for 1923
Copy of Stewardship Letter

Pictures of the ceremonies of both the removing the old stone and the laying of the new stone plus separate pictures of each item both old and new that were placed in the new stone have been arranged in a photograph album and presently is in the pastor's study for anyone who so desires to see.

This Church has owned two parsonages. The first one was purchased, already built, and first occupied in January 1922, by the family of Pastor Elbert N. Johnson. It was also the home of the families of E. Norfleet Gardner, Thomas W. Fryer and lastly by the family of S. Lewis Morgan, Jr. This parsonage was sold in August, 1946, before the present parsonage was built. Soon thereafter the S. Lewis Morgan, Jr., family moved from the first parsonage to 304 North Orange Avenue and lived there until the present parsonage was completed. Therefore, the Morgans were the last pastor family to occupy the first parsonage and the first family to occupy the present parsonage.

At a conference of this Church in August of 1947 a parsonage building program was authorized. A building committee was appointed consisting of Earl McD. Westbrook, Chairman, Paul L. Strickland, W. P. Dickey, W. M. Brannon, Mrs. C. T. Latimer, Mrs. C. L. Corbett and Mrs. Ray Horrell. On October 29, 1947, there was a letter sent out from the building committee to all members of the Church. Part of this letter is quoted: "As plans have reached the 'building' stage on the new parsonage, your committee would like to acquaint every member of the Church with the important facts in this project." "(1) A church in building a parsonage must build it large enough for any pastor's family that might ever live in it and substantial enough so that it would need few repairs during the next 50 years. A little more money spent for best materials now will save thousands of dollars over the 50 year period."

"(2) Our committee felt that in arriving at blueprint specifications we would not be satisfied to represent you without securing the technical advice of a good architect. We feel more certain of our plans as we begin to build, because our architect is one of the best obtainable."

"(3) The house is to contain four bedrooms, two size 13 x 13 and two size 13 x 15, one living room 13 x 22, dining room 13 x 15, kitchen 13 x 13, a pastor's study 13 x 13, one downstairs bathroom and two upstairs bathrooms in conjunction with the three upstairs bedrooms, a garage and a laundry room."

Soon after this letter of October 29, 1947, Turlington and Turlington, LTD., Lillington, N. C., was selected as the builder. Work began and continued skillfully with dispatch and with close attention to detail. In August, 1948, construction was complete and the Rev. S. Lewis Morgan, Jr., family were the first proud occupants of this beautiful and functional home.

Very soon now the Church will begin another major project of repairing the inside walls and redecorating the Sanctuary. The Church in conference has officially already authorized it and the funds are already in hand. Great things have been accomplished and will continue to be accomplished so long as it continues to have the competent leadership and the enthusiastic cooperation of its members that has prevailed for the past ninety-six years.

First Baptist Church

First
Baptist
Church
[Front View]

1916
or
1917

Dunn
Baptist
Church
[Wooden]
Picture
taken
in
1893

Wooden
Church
1900
After
Painting

Forground
"Hood
Home"
Paul
Hood
Riding
Bicycle
Age 7

First Parsonage - January 1922 - August 1946

Present Parsonage

Chapter V

Churches Formed By First Baptist Church

Creating new missions and later organizing new Churches whenever and wherever there is a genuine established need is a good index of the "Missionary Thrust" of a Church. This has been one commitment of the First Baptist Church, Dunn, N. C., over the years. This Church has organized five Missionary Baptist Churches in the community and at present has one mission under its wing.

SOUTH DUNN BAPTIST CHURCH

Sometime in 1908 or the early part of 1909, this Church began a "mission" in the southern area of Dunn. Later from this mission a Church was organized known as "South Dunn Baptist Church". The organization of the "South Dunn Baptist Church" caused the Dunn Baptist Church to change its name to First Baptist Church of Dunn.

On May 8, 1909, the mother Church purchased a lot from Mr. & Mrs. P. T. Massengill situated on the corner of South Magnolia Avenue and East Duke Street and erected a frame Church house for use of the newly organized Church (see real estate transaction numbers three, six and seven, Chapter II). The Sunday School for this Church for a period was held on Sunday afternoons. Some of the young people would go to the First Baptist Church Sunday School in the mornings and to Sunday School at the South Dunn Baptist Church in the afternoons.

At an annual meeting of the Little River Association held November 2, 3, 4 and 5, 1911, meeting at the Coats Baptist Church, the South Dunn Baptist sent delegates. They were J. F. Cannady, C. P. Layton and J. H. Beasley. On November 2, 1911, a petition from the South Dunn Baptist Church was read requesting membership in this association. On motion the Church was received and the delegates were given the right hand of welcome. The pastor of the South Dunn Church at that time was T. J. Hood, Goldsboro, N. C., and the Church Clerk was J. H. Beasley.

At the association annual meeting on October 31, November 1, 2, and 3, 1912, South Dunn Church was represented by letter. The pastor then was also T. J. Hood, Goldsboro, N. C., and the Church Clerk was J. H. Beasley. At the 1913 association annual meeting, the delegate was John Tart, the pastor was G. A. Bain, Buies Creek, N. C., and the Clerk was W. B. Warren. Delegates in 1914 were C. P. Layton and F. I. Houston. The pastor was G. A. Bain and the Clerk was C. P. Layton. In 1915 the delegates were W. B. Warren and C. P. Layton. The pastor was G. A. Bain and the Clerk was C. P. Layton. In 1916 the Church was not represented by delegates or letter but the pastor was still G. A. Bain, Buies Creek, N. C., and the Clerk was James Houston.

In the Little River Association annual minutes for 1917 the South Dunn Baptist Church was not listed in the roll or Churches nor in any subsequent annual minutes.

It is not known when the South Dunn Baptist Church disbanded. However, the First Baptist Church of Dunn on March 30, 1923, sold the lot and Church house that had been used by South Dunn Baptist Church to Mrs. Cassie Hodges. (See again Items Three, Six and Seven in Chapter II).

Second Baptist Church

SECOND BAPTIST CHURCH

In the latter part of 1941, Dr. Thomas W. Fryer, pastor of the First Baptist Church of Dunn and many members of the Church realized a need for a mission Sunday School in that section of Dunn then known as "Enterprise". A survey was made and the realization was confirmed. In 1942 an old store building owned by Mrs. Susan E. Tart was obtained free of charge as a place for meeting. This store building was located on "old 421" highway just beyond the Tart Lumber Mill and Cotton Gin in the section known as the "White Line". The building was torn down several years ago.

A mission Sunday School was organized in 1942 and Mr. M. B. Faircloth of the First Baptist Church was selected as the first Sunday School Superintendent. Supply preaching was done by Dr. Thomas W. Fryer, by S. Lewis Morgan, who followed Dr. Fryer as pastor of the mother Church and others until the mission was organized into a regular Church.

On Sunday, August 6, 1944, a Presbytery or organizing council was formed with Rev. S. Lewis Morgan, Jr., presiding and the Second Baptist Church was formally constituted. Those elected at this meeting to serve as officers of the new Church were Rev. E. C. Keller, pastor, M. B. Faircloth and B. O. Slaughter, Deacons, and Mrs. R. B. (Louise) Wright, Church Clerk.

Seventeen people constituted the charter membership of the new Church. They were Mr. & Mrs. E. M. Slaughter, Mr. & Mrs. B. O. Slaughter, Mrs. R. B. Wright, Mrs. Verdia Creech, Annie June Creech, Margie Creech, Rev. & Mrs. E. C. Keller, Mary Alice Keller, George Burns, Mr. & Mrs. Derwood Godwin, Marvin Slaughter, Jr., M. B. Faircloth and Mrs. J. Walter McLamb.

The newly formed Church continued to meet in the store building until their Sunday School department building could be completed. On November 2, 1945, the site on which the Church now stands was purchased from Romie Goodman for $3,500.00. This property was known as the "Isaac W. Taylor property". $750.00 of the purchase price was donated by the N. C. State Mission Board. The remaining $2,750.00 was borrowed and Dr. C. D. Bain and Herbert B. Taylor from the mother Church endorsed the note. In a Church conference on Friday, August 22, 1947, decision was made to begin construction and work soon began.

The Second Baptist Church is strong and active and the First Baptist Church is very proud of its first sustaining daughter.

North Clinton Avenue Baptist Church

NORTH CLINTON AVENUE BAPTIST CHURCH

For a number of years prior to 1952, Mr. Ernest P. Russell, Pastor, and the First Baptist Church of Dunn had been looking toward the northeast section of Dunn with the idea of beginning a branch Sunday School in that area. A survey was made as of September 30, 1961, and it was found that there were at least 109 good prospects for Sunday School available. A search began for a building to begin a mission Sunday School. It was found that Mr. Joseph Norris had a small building available at 502 North Clinton Avenue and so the First Baptist Church rented it in which to begin the Sunday School. Plans were finalized, a date set and handbills were printed and circulated. The handbill read:

The First Baptist Church
Dunn, N. C.
is opening a
Branch Sunday School
at 502 North Clinton Avenue
February 17, 1952
at 9:30 A. M.

You are cordially invited to attend. Let us think on what God's word says:
Psalms 122, Verse 1 - I was glad when they said unto me let us go into the house of the Lord.

The branch Sunday began and expanded until Mr. Norris saw a need for additional space and added an additional room to his building for another Sunday School class. The

Sunday School continued to grow and the First Baptist Church being aware of additional space requirements purchased a lot described in a deed dated March 30, 1953, located at 507 North Clinton Avenue and built what is now the educational unit of the North Clinton Avenue Baptist Church for use by this branch Sunday School. When they moved from the Norris building to their new home they were, of course, very happy and some expressed it by saying: "We are really "up town" now."

The Sunday School added a morning worship service and Mr. William Davenport was selected to be the first pastor of the mission. Upon the resignation of Mr. Davenport, Earl Davis Farthing, a student at Wake Forest College, became the pastor. Upon the resignation of Earl Davis Farthing, Joseph Creech became the Mission Pastor.

The branch Sunday School requested that the First Baptist Church, through their pastor, Ernest P. Russell, to obtain an organizational council. This was done and the minutes of this council are copied below in its entirety:

8 June 1958
2:30 P.M.

The Organization of the North Clinton Avenue Baptist Church Minutes of the Organization Council

Rev. Ernest P. Russell stated the purpose of the organizational council. The council was organized as follows:

Mr. W. E. Cobb, Moderator   W. Earl Jones, Clerk

Members from the First Baptist Church, Dunn, N. C. - Billy Hodges, Wiley Oakley, E. P. Russell, J. A. McLeod, O. O. Manning, C. D. Bain, Geo. Britton, Mr. & Mrs. Jeff Denny, Mrs. Archie Burns, Mrs. Wade Brannon. From Buies Creek Baptist Church - Julius Holloway, Associational Missionary, Robert Currin and Leon E. Davis. From Goldsboro Baptist Church - Herman Hodges.

Joseph Creech read the request and resolution hereto attached to these minutes. There being no further questions a motion was made by E. P. Russell and seconded by Jeff Denny that we proceed with the organization. Motion carried.

Rev. Joseph Creech was then officially called to be the first pastor of the North Clinton Avenue Baptist Church, Dunn, N. C. Mr. Creech accepted the call and was unanimously elected.

The remainder of the attached document was then read by several members of the new Church in its entirety.

It was agreed that members coming into the Church by July 1, 1958, will be considered charter members.

Julius Holloway then made remarks welcoming the new Church into the Little River Association.

Respectfully submitted,

W. E. Cobb, Moderator   W. Earl Jones, Clerk''

In a deed dated August 15, 1960, the First Baptist Church deeded to the North Clinton Avenue Baptist Church the lot at 507 North Clinton Avenue on which the educational building was located and described in more detail in Chapter Two, Items Eleven and Fourteen of these writings. This Church was then on its way and is making an excellent contribution to the religious life of the community.

Westfield Baptist Church

WESTFIELD BAPTIST CHURCH

Under the leadership of Dr. Tom M. Freeman, pastor of the First Baptist Church and the support of many of its members a survey was made and it was determined that there was good potential for a Church in the northwest section of the Dunn area. A meeting place was obtained for the proposed mission in the Dunn Youth Center at 901 West Broad Street. This was the former home of Mr. & Mrs. Mack M. Jernigan.

On Sunday, October 6, 1963, a mission was organized. There were twenty present for this organizational meeting including one visitor. At first the mission had only Sunday School and prayer meeting services. They met with the First Baptist Church for the morning and evening worship services and held their prayer meetings on Thursday nights so as not to conflict with the mother Church.

On Wednesday night, October 16, 1963, the First Baptist Church in conference recommended that Westfield Mission set up a building fund and voted a gift of $1,000.00 to start this fund. This fund grew very rapidly as evidenced by the speed with which it started its first building program.

Seeing a need for a permanent location for the Westfield Mission, should it be constituted a Church, Mr. Walter H. Adams, unmarried, executed a "deed of gift" dated November 1, 1963, to First Baptist Church a tract of land consisting of 6.89 acres located on Old Coats Road for use as building site for "Westfield". After Westfield Baptist Church was constituted the mother Church deeded on July 22, 1964, to the Westfield Baptist Church this same tract of land. (See Items Fifteen, Sixteen and Seventeen - Chapter II).

Morning worship services began on January 5, 1964. Mr. Bobby Barefoot, Senior Ministerial Student, was called and served as the first "Mission" Pastor on a part-time basis. Upon the resignation of Rev. Barefoot, the Church called in September, 1965, Rev. Roger Patterson to be its first full-time pastor.

The Mission was constituted "Westfield Baptist Church" on June 28, 1964, with 41 charter members and 6 candidates for Baptism. Dr. Casper C. Warren preached the sermon on that day. At the time the Church was formed the Sunday School had and enrollment of 100 members.

The first building program of this Church began in the early fall of 1964 and they moved from the Dunn Youth Center into this new building in November, 1964. This first building still stands behind the present Church building near the back of the lot and remained their meeting place from November, 1964, until they moved into their present Church building in February, 1967.

Faith Baptist Church

FAITH BAPTIST CHURCH

The officials of the Little River Baptist Association and the Johnston Baptist Association jointly appeared to see a need for a Baptist Mission in the Mary Stewart community on U. S. Highway 301 north of Dunn, N. C. A joint survey committee was formed and first met on April 11, 1970, at the "Gladys Restaurant" near Mary Stewart School. Members of this committee were: Rev. Thomas M. Freeman, Pastor, First Baptist Church of Dunn; Rev. Harold Mitchell, Pastor, Benson Baptist Church; Rev. Everett Marion, Moderator of the Little River Association; Mr. C. Blake Thomas, Moderator of the Johnston Association; Rev. Julius Holloway, Missionary of Little River Association; Rev. R. E. Moore, Missionary of Johnston Association; Mr. Oliver O. Manning from First Baptist Church of Dunn and Mr. Jonah Caudle, a local layman.

The community survey that followed indicated a very favorable and promising situation. A small dwelling house owned by Mrs. Letha Dunn, Benson, N. C., was secured as a meeting place for the mission. Mrs. Dunn gladly loaned it rent free. The name of the Mission agreed upon was "Johnston-Harnett Mission"

A Sunday School was formed and met for the first time on June 21, 1970. It was finally decided at this meeting to conduct a vacation Bible school under the joint effort of the

Benson Baptist Church and the First Baptist Church of Dunn. The school was held beginning Monday, June 22, and continued through Saturday, June 27, 1970, and proved very successful. Attendance at Sunday School on June 28, 1970, was 23 and the collection was $66.09. Worship service also began this same day and the first mission pastor was Rev. George Ware.

Sunday School and worship service continued regularly and the growth pattern was encouraging. On May 30, 1972, it was decided to change the mission name to "Faith Baptist Mission".

A building fund was commenced as a means for purchasing a site and constructing a building. A site was purchased for $10,000.00 consisting of 3.9 acres from Mr. & Mrs. Floyd L. Altman and Mr. Altman presented the deed to the mission on October 29, 1972. A dedication of the lot was held the same day at the land site led by Rev. Julius Holloway, Superintendent of Missions Little River Association.

After the land had been fully paid for, ground breaking for a new building was held on June 24, 1973. The ceremony was led by Rev. Julius Holloway, assisted by Dr. Thomas M. Freeman, Pastor, First Baptist Church of Dunn and Rev. Don Price, Pastor of Benson Baptist Church. There was thirty-two people in attendance. Mr. Gordon Smith was employed as building contractor and construction began immediately. The new building is 80 ft. x 36 ft. and contains a sanctuary with choir area and Baptistry, seven Sunday school rooms, nursery and kitchen.

The first worship service held in the new building was on Thanksgiving Day, November 22, 1973. The building was not complete and some of the outside doors had not been hung. Rev. Julius Hollowell was pastor. Dedication of the new building occurred on November 10, 1974. The last $6,000.00 note was later paid off and the ceremony of burning the notes took place on October 19, 1975. Total cost of both the land and building amounted to $89,937.15.

A Presbytery or advisory council consisting of Rev. Jefrie Davis, Dr. Thomas M. Freeman, Rev. Julius Holloway and others was formed at 2:00 P.M. on Sunday, October 21, 1979, and the Church was regularly constituted under the name of "Faith Baptist Church". The Church is growing and prospering. Consideration is being given to building a fellowship hall. The First Baptist Church of Dunn is very proud of its youngest daughter.

THE CRESTVIEW BAPTIST MISSION

The idea of a Baptist Mission began with several people living in the area of Spiveys Corner in Sampson County on Highway 421 about eleven miles south of Dunn, N. C. As a result during the summer of 1962 Rev. Gary Long, Pastor of Spring Branch Baptist Church conducted a tent revival in this area which stimulated additional interest. Mission Committees from the First Baptist Church of Dunn and Spring Branch Church jointly discussed the need for a missionary Baptist Mission in the area.

In the winter of 1963-1964 neighborhood prayer meetings began to meet on Thursday nights in one of the homes of the community. The name "Crestview" was decided at these prayer meetings. A building fund was also started in an effort to select a site and construct a building for a meeting place for the prayer meetings and to organize a Sunday School. The minutes of a Church conference of the First Baptist Church of Dunn held December 18, 1963, include this statement: "that we approve continuing efforts of the Church Mission Committee to work with the Spring Branch Church in trying to establish a mission Sunday school in the area of Spiveys Corner on Highway 421 East and that we approve the effort of the committee to secure a site and meeting place."

Accordingly, a Board of Trustees was set up composed of M. M. Jernigan, O. O. Manning, W. E. Cobb and Sam Judge from First Baptist Church of Dunn and Thomas Henry Hinson, Thad H. Dixon and Casper Phillips from Spring Branch Baptist Church. A site was located and purchased on the west side of Highway 421 at the junction of N. C. Highway 242 about two miles north of Spiveys Corner. On Sunday, May 15, 1966, ground was broken for the beginning of a modest building program.

Over the years this mission has had its high peaks and low dells but continues to function. Recently, another small addition has been added to the original Sunday School unit. In addition to Sunday School, morning worship services are held on a regular basis. It is hoped that a growth pattern and independent financial stability will be reached so that this mission can be some day constituted into a regular missionary Baptist Church.

74

Chapter VI

Unrelated Events

It appears fitting, especially in a Church history, that a division in the writing should be set aside for events or happenings that would not normally fall in any chapter heading but could be classified as historical "goodies" or maybe sometimes not so good and yet constitute history just the same. Factual histories of anything are never all good or all bad but in the aggregate make up the sum total of the subject at hand.

The events in this chapter may not be necessarily in chronological order but will likely be recorded for the most part as patient and persistant digging bring them to "light". It may be said by some after reading this chapter: "What a conglomerate of unrelated events!"

First Communion Set

On June 30, 1887, Rev. J. M. Beasley on behalf of his devoted wife presented to the Dunn Baptist Church a silver mounted communion set. The set consisted of a large silver pitcher, two large silver goblets and two silver bread trays. The container in which they were stored when not in use was a portable mahogany cabinet closely resembling a little house. The cabinet has been sometime through the years lost or destroyed.

Rev. and Mrs. J. M. Beasley were the parents of Mrs. James Addison Taylor and the great grandparents of Mrs. Emma Ann Taylor Ruark. Rev. Beasley owned a leading jewelry store in his home town of Fayetteville, North

Carolina. This is the same J. M. Beasley referred to in the early part of Chapter I who organized "Antioch Baptist Church" in Cumberland County, was instrumental in building its first Church house and was the Church's first pastor.

In later years when the Dunn Baptist Church purchased a more modern communion set with individual cups, the Church voted to give the original set to Mrs. James Addison Taylor, daughter of Mr. & Mrs. Beasley. This original set has been passed down from generation to generation until now it is in the proud possession of Mrs. Emma Ann Taylor Ruark.

The following quote is taken from the minutes of a regular Church conference of this Church on June 11, 1891: "The Church adopted a constitution, rules of decorum and by-laws - which see in printed pamphlet." The few Church records that are available to this writer do not show that this action has been, before 1978, rescinded. However, copies of these documents have not been found and this Church has not governed itself by them for at least thirty-five years. This is the second constitution. The first one was adopted the day the Church was organized on September 27, 1885. In a regular Church conference on August 27, 1978, the third constitution and by-laws was adopted which automatically rescinded the ones of 1891 and govern the actions of the Church presently. The present constitution and by-laws are found in the appendix of this work.

From about 1891 and for many years thereafter the roll of the Church was called at every Church conference and each absentee recorded. At some conferences members were called up for dancing, business transactions unbecoming a Christian, cursing, drinking, etc. Reprimands were a common practice and an occasional expulsion was meted out in extreme cases.

There is an article printed in "The Little River Record" Buies Creek Academy, Buies Creek, N. C., July, 1916, Volume XVII, No. 9. The article was written by Mrs. E. A. Harper and deals with some facts about the work of the "Ladies Aid Society" of Dunn Baptist Church. Part of this article reads thus: "In 1913 the Society decided to buy a pipe organ for the new Church to cost $2,500.00, half of that amount to be paid by Mr. Carnegie."

"Through the kindness of Mr. J. L. Hatcher and Mr. Jno. A. McKay we were given the use of a room on Main Street which we used as an exchange, which we opened in March 1913. We divided our ladies into four groups, each group having a chairman, and working in turn one group each Saturday. We raised $800.00 in a little more than a year and on August 24, 1914, the pipe organ committee, Mrs. Hatcher, Mrs. Pittman, Mrs. Hines and Mrs. Long, met in Mr. Clifford's office and signed a note for $450.00 to meet our obligation with the Estley Organ Company."

"On September 1, 1915, the same committee met in the Church to receive the organ after it was installed."

"On September 15, 1915, the last note was paid cancelling the debt. Messrs. James A. Taylor, J. W. Draughon, J. C. Clifford and G. F. Pope became endorsers on these notes."

The chimes were not a part of the original organ. In 1946 the Richard Warren family donated the set of chimes which were made a part of the original organ and carried forward to the new organ.

The following is found in the minutes of a Deacon's Meeting held February 11, 1946. "Mr. S. L. Morgan reported for committee on chimes which met with Mr. Stevens and his helpers. The contract was signed and chimes are being made ready for installation". The minutes of a Deacon's Meeting held April 16, 1946, bears this statement: "Mr. Lewis Morgan reported that the chimes were ready for installation." The dedication service for the chimes was held on Sunday evening, July 28, 1946. Dr. Casper Warren preached the dedicatory sermon. The dedication service bulletin reads in part as follows: "The Warren Memorial Chimes are presented in memory of Mr. & Mrs. R. M. Warren and daughter, Cora Warren Denning, by their family, Mrs. Mary Warren (H.T.) Stevens, Mrs. Marguerite Warren (G. T., Jr.) Noel, Dr. Casper Warren, Mr. J. O. Warren, Mr. Ralph N. Warren, Mr. Russell Warren, Mr. R. L. Denning.

It was recognized by the music committee as early as 1956 that the Church organ was due much needed repairs and modernization. Under the capable leadership of the nineteenth pastor, Rev. Ernest P. Russell, a fund raising program was started which was most successful. Accordingly, in the Church Conference of July 27, 1958, a contract was authorized to make the needed repairs to electrify the console and to move the console from the choir section to its present location. The contract was awarded to J. Vernon Suitt, Proprietor, Durham Organ Service, R5, Box 421, Durham, N. C., at a cost of $4,465.00. Repairs were begun in 1958 and completed in 1959.

About sixteen or seventeen years after the organ had been repaired and remodeled it began to badly deteriorate and major repairs were determined not to be the answer. It was, therefore, decided to begin a fund raising program and monies began to come in. Mr. Mack M. Jernigan, realizing that a new organ was needed now, on March 2, 1979, presented to the First Baptist Church a check in the amount of $50,000.00 to be used for the purchase of a new pipe organ. In his letter to the Church in which the check was enclosed he said in part: "I am giving this for the glory of God and in loving honor of my wife, Sallie Naylor Jernigan, who has been connected with the music of this Church for more than 50 years."

Reasonably soon after receipt of the check a contract was given to William Zimmer and Sons, Charlotte, North Carolina, to design, build and install the organ. It required approximately two years to build. The console and many pipes from the old organ were reworked and reused in the new organ. The chimes were also reused. On January 12, 1981, the remainder of the old organ was dismantled and work began on the empty chamber to prepare for its reception of the new organ.

The new organ was first played for a morning worship service on March 15, 1981. This is a quote from the Church Bulletin dated March 15, 1981: "Our new organ is being used in our worship today for the first time". (Mrs. Taylor Newton was the organist). Plans were made for a dedication service which was held at the evening worship service on Sunday, April 26, 1981. A most accomplished organist, Mr. Thomas E. Hawley, Jr., gave the organ recital. It might be of value here to say that Mr. Hawley grew up in and under the influence of this Church.

A segment of the litany of dedication is recorded here: "in a spirit of humility, praise and Thanksgiving, we come to dedicate this organ. We are thankful to God for His blessings. We are thankful to all who have prayed and worked to make this day possible. We are thankful for the faith, love and generosity of Mr. Mack M. Jernigan, who has

given this organg to our Church, and to Mrs. Sallie Naylor
Jernigan, who inspired the gift and in whose honor it was
given, to the glory of God and for use in the praise and
worship of God.''

First Organ

The organ of 1915 and the one of 1981 were not the only
two organs the Church has owned. In March, 1907, the
''Ladies Aid Society'' of the Church purchased an organ
through Darins Eatman at a cost of $75.49. This was an
organ that was pumped by the feet of the organist to provide
wind pressure while she played on the keyboard. When the
Church moved into the brick building in December, 1914, this
organ was moved into the new sanctuary and used until the
pipe organ was completed and accepted on September 1,
1915. The little organ was moved then into Sunday school
departments and continued in use until it gave out then
moved again into the basement furnace room.

Some years later after the organ was covered in coal
dust and soot it was decided to have a ''Clean-Up Day''. The
little organ was about to find its last resting place on a trash
dump. For sentimental reasons, Mr. Herbert B. Taylor asked
for it and moved it to his insurance office downtown. There is
found a resting place again until about thirty years ago, Mr.
Taylor's daughter, Mrs. Emma Ann Ruark, developed the
idea that it could be converted by a competent cabinet maker
into a useful piece of furniture. Today it is a beautiful desk
and sits in a hallowed spot in the home of Mrs. Ruark.

It may be of interest to give a sidelight to this little organ. Sometime between December, 1914, and September, 1915, when it was being used in the sanctuary of the brick Church, while Mrs. James Addison Taylor, was playing it for a regular worship service she had a very sudden and very serious stroke from which she never fully recovered until her death on February 2, 1933.

The December Church Bulletin dated December 6, 1931, has the following statement under "Items of Interest":

"At the November conference of the Church the following resolution, which had been on the table for two months, was taken up and passed unanimously. RESOLUTION ON CHURCH MEMBERS WHO FORSAKE THE ASSEMBLING OF THEMSELVES TOGETHER. Inasmuch as we are warned in God's word against forsaking the assembling of ourselves together; and inasmuch as in our covenant we pledged to support the services of the Church by our presence; and inasmuch as it is sadly that some utterly ignore this important claim of the Church, we, the members of the First Baptist Church of Dunn, in conference assembled November 4, 1931, resolve that if a resident, physically well member absents himself for an entire year from all services, he shall be cited by the Deacons to appear before the Church in its January conference to give reason for his absence. In the failure of said member to furnish proper excuse, his name shall be dropped from the roll of the Church, the grounds for his expulsion being indifference to the work of the Kingdom in the local Church."

All organizations and especially Churches have their very high peaks and very low dells. This Church is no exception. The purposes this writer has for including and recording this segment is, first it is a part of this Church history and second to demonstrate that regardless of how low a group of believers who trust in the Divine will and purpose of God, the power of prayer, the recognition of human misgivings and a determination to strive together for His Divine Glory can go and still obtain victory and spiritually profit thereby not only as an individual but as a corporate body in Christ.

This lowest point came between the fall of 1914 and the mid-summer of 1917. Fright, extremely low morale, financial distress and human bickering possessed the congregation during that period. World War I began in Europe about the time that the brick Church was started and that in itself was most upsetting. The April 1922 Bulletin reads in part as follows: "Our Church home which we now dedicate to God was begun in 1913, following a resolution of our Church timidly passed that we undertake the erection of a new building costing approximately $15,000.00."

"Accordingly an architect was employed, plans were adopted and work begun with a little faith, no cash and a subscription list of about $12,000.00. Of course, we knew that the plan adopted could not be carried to completion for the amount limited in the initial resolution, but if our eyes had been opened to the fact that we were beginning the erection of a building that would cost us $45,000.00, I am sure we should have failed completely; yet, though I cannot tell how it was done, that is the sum which we finally placed in the building."

"Perhaps the most trying ordeal through which we passed, was the fright which we had to overcome when our building was half done and our debt hardly touched, the storm of the World War closed all markets, paralyzed credits, tested our faith and challenged our courage as nothing else had done."

The pastor, Rev. James Long, who began his ministry in this Church on February 1, 1912, and who resigned in November, 1914, was here during the planning and construction, left this pastorate just one month before any part of the new Church was occupied. It is recorded in some writings other than Church records that Rev. Long resigned and left under extreme pressure and declared that he would never set foot in any part of the completed and occupied building.

Following the resignation of Rev. James Long, the Church extended a call to Dr. W. R. Cullom, who was pastor immediately prior to Rev. Long. Dr. Cullom declined the pastorial call but obligated himself to preach two Sundays per month and to assume the responsibility of getting someone else to preach the other two Sundays until a pastor could be obtained.

About a year after Dr. Cullom began this interim pastorate he realized an immediate urgent need for some outside financial assistance and, therefore, he personally circulated among more than one hundred of his friends and acquaintances a "Statement and A Request" which is quoted in its entirety:

"A STATEMENT AND A REQUEST"

"Something over a year ago the First Baptist Church of Dunn, N. C., asked me to supply their pulpit for a while and try and help them out of a trying situation. Their situation was this: About two years before that time they voted to build a house of worship that should cost $15,000.00 and certainly not more than $20,000.00 - Soon after the war broke out in Europe they found themselves with a house that had cost over $30,000.00 with a debt of about $18,000.00 on them and the house still unfinished. I have not allowed myself to be too critical as to who was responsible for this condition of affairs. My purpose has been and is not to grumble at them for being in this plight but to help them out of it."

"With financial conditions as they have been for the past two years, many a Church in their circumstances would have gone to pieces in a panic, they have held together remarkably well. Their membership has increased by about fifty; their Sunday School has grown quite a bit; they have a good Senior and Junior B.Y.P.U.; they have put a new piano into their Sunday School, they have put new pews into the Church at a cost of nearly $2,000.00, most of which has been paid; and they reduced their debt by more than $6,000.00. This Church has a fine body of young people in it, and with proper care should soon become one of the stronger Churches of the State."

"Three tasks are pressing heavily upon them for the coming fall. They are these: (1) Between five and six thousand dollars on their debt will be due before Christmas; (2) a heating plant is an indispensable necessity if their beautiful building is to be taken care of; (3) the basement should by all means be finished up both because the Sunday School is suffering for more room, and because this would enable them to save the new pews in a way that will otherwise be impossible."

"They have never gone to the outside world for help nor are they going to do so in any general way. We are hoping that we can get one hundred of our friends to join the pastor in giving $10.00 each for putting in the heating plant which it is estimated to cost about $1,000.00. If the other ninety-eight are secured, may I draw on you on October 1st for this amount? If I can bring this to pass for them I believe they can arrange to manage the balance themselves. But they do have just a little more for this fall then they can get through with without a little outside help. Please think and pray over the matter and let me hear from you as soon as you can."

W. R. Cullom, Acting Pastor
Wake Forest, N. C.

.The new pews were contracted for about a year before I began my supply work.

W.R.C.

Dr. Cullom secured the services of Dr. Balus Cabe and together these two Godly men supplied as interim pastors and led the faithful flock from November, 1914, until June, 1917, through clouds of doubt, fear and frustration to see the light and sunshine of a new day.

The next regular pastor was Rev. John A. Ellis who served from July 1, 1917, until January 27, 1918, and resigned to enter the service of his country during the latter part of World War I as a Chaplain in the U. S. Army. The next pastor was Rev. Eugene I. Oliver, who came on June 2, 1918, and remained until June, 1921. The Church had recovered and was on to greater service. Somehow and in some way the total debt was liquidated in a period of less than eight years and the notes were burned on April 2, 1922. SOME SAY A MIRACLE WAS WORKED"

The first known Church monthly bulletin was printed and distributed on October 6, 1918. Rev. Eugene I. Olive, who was single at that time and who later married the choir director, Miss Ina Pearson on June 29, 1926, was pastor. It records the Church officers and the Board of Deacons. There is also listed the names of men from this Church who were at that time in military service during World War I. Regular services of the Church with dates and hour of meeting for the month of October, 1918, are noted. Among them were Sunday School, morning worship, evening worship, prayer meeting, Senior B.Y.P.U., Junior B.Y.P.U., Board of Deacons, Church Conference, Communion Service, W.M.S., Ladies Aid Society, Sunbeams and Workers Conference.

Among the "Items of Interest" is an expression of thanks from the bachelor pastor and because it is somewhat of a human interest story, part of it is quoted: "When it was known that he was to begin housekeeping, there fell upon him at the hands of the ladies a bounteous shower. When he was making ready to sit down at his own table, the Ladies Aid presented him with more dishes than he had food to fill. Shortly after the dishes had been tried, the men and the women pounded him with more food than he had dishes to contain. When the nights grew cool, the Y.W.A. handed him a quilt with the promise of others as the temperature should give rise to the need. All the favors you have shown make him feel very unworthy. In deepest humility he resolved to endeavor to show in unselfish service the gratitude his heart feels."

In 1972, the Church bought a lot on which was located two dwelling houses plus outbuildings, etc, known as the "Poole property". Before this lot could be developed into what is now an excellent recreation area, it was necessary to dispose of these buildings and other attachments. An auction sale was agreed upon. In the minutes of a Church Conference held March 14, 1973, it is recorded that H. Paul Strickland reported on the sale of the houses and equipment on the Poole property and that the total amount of the sale was $1,555.00.

In the 1860's or 1870's there was a water mill on Black River near where the new sewage treatment plant has been completed behind the present Betsy Johnson Memorial Hospital. Flood waters developed on the river and washed the mill away, leaving only a part of the frame of the mill still standing. The dam deteriorated and soon also washed away but the waters around this old mill site proved a good place for a "swimming hole". The place became known as "old frame" and was used as the First Baptismal site for the newly formed Baptist Church. Due to the fact that "Gainey's Bridge" on Black River downstream from "old frame" was more accessible, the Baptismal site was changed to "Gainey's Bridge". Later the Baptismal site was moved to "Surles Pond", now known as "Hanna's Pond" and remained there until the wooden Church was built which included a Baptistry. It may be of interest to know that the Baptistry in the wooden Church was under the floor where the choir sat. When Baptisms took place, part of the choir chairs were removed and the floor thrown open on hinges like a double door, exposing the Baptistry.

Church budgets are in some measure a partial indication of Church growth and for this reason some figures as to budget size are listed:

Budget for 1935 - 1936	$ 7,000.00
for 1945 - 1946	$ 14,775.00
for 1950 - 1951	$ 23,637.20
for 1980	$145,000.00
for 1981	$165,100.00

In addition to the regular budget, special offerings were made each year for the "Annie Armstrong Home Missions", "Lottie Moon Foreign Missions", "State Missions", "Care for the Aging", "Children's Home", "World Hunger", etc.

In the minutes of Diaconate held August 4, 1944, there is a statement: "Recommendation to Church by Diaconate to consolidate the Board of Deacons and also the Board of Deconesses into one single board to be known as the Diaconate, all of whom shall, for the sake of convenience, be referred to as Deacons."

This Church has had many Revival Services, most of which brought many conversions and other types of Church additions. Spiritual renewal and renewed activity by Church members also were usually quite evident. As an example, statements from three former revivals appear below.

In the minutes of a Church Conference held June 18, 1906, there is recorded: "A series of meetings conducted by the pastor Bro. W. R. Cullom, assisted by Bro. Fred N. Day, of Winston-Salem, N. C., begun the 4th day of June, was closed today the 18th. The doors of the Church were opened from day to day and the following members were added to the Church."

After this statement sixty-five (65) names were separately listed. Of this 65 names, ten had for some reason been lined out. There remained 55 names. Three were on statement of faith and former Baptism, 25 came as candidates for Baptism and 27 came by letter from other Churches.

There is found this statement in the minutes of a Church Conference held March 18, 1908: "A series of meetings conducted by the pastor, W. R. Cullom, assisted by Bro. Neighbors of Salisbury, N. C., beginning . . . . . The doors of the Church were opened from day to day for the reception of members and the following members were added to the Church."

After the above statement 35 names were listed. One of them was lined out leaving 34. One came by restoration, two by free will, five by letter and twenty-six for Baptism.

During the pastorate of Dr. E. Norfleet Gardner, the Church Bulletin for March, 1938, dated March 6, 1938, is copied in part: "Our people were much in prayer and joyful anticipation before Carey Barker of Lynchburg returned for his second meeting in Dunn. During his stay of two weeks in our midst we were impelled every day to express gratitude that God had led him our way. Since his leaving we have served more joyfully in the task of our Lord. Let us continue to ask God to watch over him, and bless his ministry."

"One hundred accessions to the Church was one result of his stay in Dunn. To those whose names have not been mentioned in a previous bulletin, we extend a hearty WELCOME."

Following this statement sixty names are listed as candidates for Baptism, twenty-five names received by letter, and five names received by statement. In the week previous to the meeting ten were added to the Church. These were evidentally included with those at the meeting to make the one hundred. Just think! One hundred members at one time!

This Church has had three official names. When it was constituted on September 27, 1885, it was named that day "Greenwood Baptist Church". When it moved into the City Limits of Dunn in 1887 the name was changed to "Dunn Baptist Church". On organizing a Church, about 1909, in the southern part of the Dunn area, the name was changed to "First Baptist Church". Regardless of the name, this Church has always conducted itself with sincerity, humbleness, and dedication to the worship and service of God Himself and in spreading the Good News of our risen and living Christ not only in this community but to those even unto the uttermost parts of the Earth.

BIBLIOGRAPHY

Records of First Baptist Church of Dunn, N. C.

Records and Histories by Herbert B. Taylor

History of Dunn Baptist Church by J. C. Clifford

History of First Baptist Church by Dr. Baylus Cabe

A History of Cool Springs Baptist Church, Sanford, N. C.

A History of Hood Memorial Christian Church, Dunn, N. C.

A History of First Baptist Church, Gastonia, N. C.

Harnett County Register of Deeds

Harnett County Board of Education, Lillington, N. C.

Harnett County Library, Lillington, N. C.

Dunn City Library, Dunn, N. C.

Fayetteville City Library, Fayetteville, N. C.

N. C. Supreme Court Library, Raleigh, N. C.

Campbell University Library, Buies Creek, N. C.

Wake Forest University Library, Winston Salem, N. C.

Dunn City Directories

New South River Baptist Association, Fayetteville, N. C.

South River Baptist Association Minute Books

Little River Baptist Association Minute Books

Official Records, including maps, fire department records, etc., City of Dunn, N. C.

Historial Research Records by Mrs. Lina S. Ennis

"The Little River Record", published by Dr. J. A. Campbell - April, 1898, to July, 1918

"The Dunn Dispatch", Dunn, N. C.

"The Daily Record", Dunn, N. C.

The Biblical Recorder

Charity and Children

"The Sampsonian", Clinton, N. C.

"The Gastonia Daily Gazette", Gastonia, N. C.

Personal interviews with many, many people but especially with Mrs. Emma Ann Ruark, George W. Williams, Mrs. Louise P. Stewart, Dr. Thomas M. Freeman, Rev. Ernest P. Russell, Graham Henry, H. Paul Strickland, Dr. Robert A. Jordan, Rev. Coley Rock

Records of North Clinton Avenue Baptist Church, Dunn, N. C.

Records of Second Baptist Church, Dunn, N. C.

Records of Westfield Baptist Church, Dunn, N. C.

Records of Faith Baptist Church, Dunn, N. C.

"Depth Study of A Local Church Program - First Baptist Church, Dunn, N. C." by Miss Nancy Parrish - May, 1967 (Campbell College Student Research Paper)

N. C. Department of Archives and History

Turlington and Turlington, LTD., Lillington, N. C.

Southern Baptist Foreign Mission Board, Richmond, Va.

Virginia Baptist Historical Society and Boatwright Memorial Library, University of Richmond, Richmond, Va.

North Carolina Baptist State Convention Headquarters, Raleigh, N. C.

Offices of North Carolina Grand Lodge of Masons, Raleigh, N. C.

Offices of Virginia Grand Lodge of Masons, Richmond, Virginia

Alexandria and Washington Lodge No. 22 A. F. & A. M., Alexandria, Virginia

90

Appendix

At least ten (10) of the former members of this Church have become ordained ministers and have distinguished themselves in their chosen fields of service.

Albert B. Harrell
John Brainard Taylor
T. Sloan Guy, Sr.
Dr. Casper C. Warren
William A. Poole
Robert J. Barefoot
Clarence L. Corbett, Jr.
Bennie Wood
Jerry Barfield
Earl Davis Farthing

Earl Davis Farthing has also served on the foreign fields as a missionary, having served a tour of duty in Japan.

RESIDENT MEMBERS
FIRST BAPTIST CHURCH, DUNN, N. C.
August 27, 1981

Adams, Mrs. Arthur
Aldredge, Emmett C., Jr.
Aldredge, Mrs. Carla
Aldredge, Mrs. Emmett C., Sr.
Allen, Mrs. Callie E.
Allred, Leonard
Allred, Mrs. Myrtle
Atkins, Bennie F.
Atkins, Mrs. Johnnie Mae
Ausley, Sam H., Jr.
Ausley, Mrs. Elizabeth
Avery, Mrs. Glenn (Barbara T.)
Aycock, Mrs. C. B. (Cleda)
Bagley, Mrs. Barbara
Bagley, Cindy
Barbour, Ellis Carl
Barbour, Mrs. Ginger
Barbour, Mrs. Fred
Barbour, Wayne T.
Barbour, Mrs. Mary Sue
Barefoot, Mrs. Bernard (Lillian)
Barefoot, Mrs. Carol
Barefoot, Brian
Barefoot, Mike
Barefoot. Scott

Barefoot, Mrs. Carlton (Verle)
Barefoot, Mrs. Troy (Lida)
Barefoot, Mac
Barefoot, Mrs. Louise
Barfield, Carey B.
Barfield, Mrs. Rosa
Barfield, Mrs. W. E. (Ruth)
Barfield, Wm. P.
Barfield, Mrs. Annette
Barrett, George
Barrett, Mrs. Hermie
Barrow, Mrs. Royce (Ann Luto)
Bass, Howard
Bass, Daisy
Bates, William, Jr. (Billy)
Bates, Mrs. Patricia
Batts, Jackie Ray
Batts, Mrs. Catherine
Beach, Mrs. Dan (Ella)
Beasley, Mrs. Jeffrey A. (Bren)
Beasley, Wallace
Beasley, Mrs. Darleen
Beasley, Wayne
Best, Braxton B.
Best, Mrs. Grace

Best, Brooks
Best, Mrs. Debbie
Bischoff, Mrs. Eloise
Blake, Mrs. Elizabeth
Bowen, Wiley
Bowen, Mrs. Peggy
Bowen, Rebecca
Boyette, Dennis
Boyette, Mrs. Eloise
Boyette, Flo
Boyette, Edwin
Boyette, Mrs. Beatrice
Boyette, Frances
Brannan, Mrs. W. M.
Brewer, Mrs. Ruth
Britton, Mrs. George (Elizabeth)
Brown, Mrs. James C.
Brown, Leisa
Brown, Chris
Bryan, Mrs. Irene
Buell, Jesse B.
Buell, Mrs. Linda
Buell, Mrs. Silas
Butler, McCauley
Butler, Mrs. Vera
Byrd, Bruce
Byrd, Mrs. Barbara
Byrd, Carl
Byrd, Mrs. Dan
Byrd, Mrs. Walter F.
Campbell, Mrs. Joseph T. (Linda)
Campbell, Bill
Campbell, Deborah
Campbell, Joseph Thomas, Jr.
Campbell, Mrs. Locke
Campbell, Lockwood
Campbell, Mrs. Mary
Cannady, Howard
Cannady, Mrs. Shirley
Cannady, Jennifer
Cannady, Jeanne
Cannady, James F.
Cannady, Mrs. Joyce
Cannady, Elizabeth Hope
Cannady, James Matthew
Capps, Lewis
Capps, Mrs. Carolyn
Capps, Lisa

Capps, Gregg
Carr, Richard J.
Carr, Mrs. Doris
Carr, Bryan
Carr, Jenny
Carr, Robert B.
Carr, Mrs. Loray
Carr, Angela
Carr, Emily
Carroll, Mrs. Herbert M.
Cashwell, Mrs. Irene
Catlett, Mrs. Davis C. (Clara)
Ciccone, Mrs. John (Dorothy)
Coats, Mrs. Hazel
Coats, James R.
Coats, Mrs. Patricia
Coats, Scott
Coats, Kimberly
Coats, Ralph
Coats, L. L. Sr.
Coats, Mrs. Ann
Coates, Wesley
Coates, Mrs. Alice
Cobb, Alton, A.
Cobb, Mrs. W. E. (Pressie)
Coleman, David F.
Coleman, Mrs. Carolyn
Coleman, Dava
Cooper, Mrs. Ruth D.
Cooper, Wm. C., Sr.
Corbett, Mrs. C. L. (Mildred)
Corbin, Mrs. Thomas J.
Corbin, Tommy
Cox, Glenn, Jr.
Cox, Glenn, Sr.
Cox, Mrs. Marcella
Cox, Connie
Connor, Mrs. C. T. (Ruth)
Creech, Mrs. F. W. (Betty)
Creed, B. G.
Creed, Mrs. Linda
Creed, Chris
Creed, Clint
Crumpler, Royce
Crumpler, Mrs. Frankie
Crumpler, Wanda
Crumpler, Diane
Culp, Miss Amanda

Daniels, W. Ray
Daniels, Mrs. Lib
Daniels, Kim
Daniels, John
Davis, Donald W.
Davis, Mrs. Kathleen
Davis, Aprile
Davis, Krystal
Davis, Neal E.
Davis, Mrs. Jane
Dawson, J. M.
Denning, Miss Edna
Denning, Miss Lola
Dixon, James Roland
Dixon, Mrs. Millard (Dorothy)
Dixon, Jerry Stephen (Steve)
Dixon, Jonathan
Dorman, Mrs. Russell B.
Dorman, Gale
Drew, Mrs. Don Ella
Drew, Paul B.
Driver, Eugene
Driver, Mrs. Mary Lou
Dudley, Willard H.
Dudley, Mrs. Hilda
Duncan, R. Haruz
Duncan, Mrs. Myrtle
Edens, Edward Glenn, Jr. (Eddie)
Edens, Dana Renee
Edwards, Joseph E.
Edwards, Phyllis
Eldridge, Alan
Eldridge, Harvey, Jr.
Eldridge, Mrs. Tense
Eldridge, Steven
Elmore, Mrs. James (Elgeree)
Elmore, Cynthia
Elmore, Johnny
Ennis, Mrs. Curtis (Lina)
Ennis, Mrs. Elsie
Ennis, Mrs. H. L. (Pauline)
Earp, Bobby
Earp, Mrs. Marinda
Earp, Hal
Earp, Dee Ann
Ennis, Raymond
Ennis, Mrs. Audrey
Ennis, R. O. (Bill)

Ennis, Mrs. Pearl
Ennis, Thomas Ray
Farthing, Mrs. James, Sr.
Farthing, James S., Jr.
Farthing, Mrs. Rosalyn
Farthing, Lucille
Fennell, Mrs. Ann
Fennell, Lori
Fennell, William C., Jr.
Finch, Keith G., Jr.
Finch, Mrs. Anne Arnold
Finch, Keith G., Sr.
Finch, Mrs. Virginia
Fisher, Mrs. Chas. Ray (Ann)
Freda, James Anthony
Freeman, Thomas M.
Freeman, Mrs. Maisie
Fuller, Kenneth M.
Fuller, Mrs. Linda
Fowler, Charles
Fowler, Mrs. Nita
Fowler, Michele
Fowler, Melanie
Fowler, Tony
Gagich, Mrs. Danny
Gavin, Mrs. Lewis (Annie Rose)
Godwin, Alton Edward
Godwin, Mrs. Dovie
Godwin, Dewey
Godwin, H. E. (Tommy)
Godwin, Locke
Godwin, J. Leon
Godwin, Mrs. Mae
Godwin, J. Leon, Jr.
Godwin, Joseph H.
Godwin, Mrs. Christine
Gomez, E. N. (Henry)
Gomez, Mrs. Norma
Gomez, Lisa
Grace, Robert A.
Grace, Mrs. Carolyn
Grace, John Robert
Green, Herman P.
Green, Mrs. Elizabeth
Grimes, Mrs. Eunice
Hall, James W.
Hall, Mrs. Myrtle
Hall, Bill

Hancock, Mrs. Norma Jean
Harant, Mrs. Frankie
Hardison, Mrs. David A. (Oma C.)
Hardison, Franklin
Hardison, Mrs. Kenneth
Hawley, Miss Fannie
Hawley, James E.
Hawley, Mrs. Jessie
Hawley, Thomas Earl, Sr.
Hawley, Mrs. Jewel
Hayes, Jack
Hayes, Mrs. Elsie U.
Hames, Don
Hallman, Thomas Bryan, III
Hallman, Mrs. Cheryl
Henry, Mrs. George W.
Henry, R. Graham
Henry, Mrs. Margaret
Henry, George William
Herring, J. T.
Herring, Mrs. Ilee
Hinson, Mrs. A. T. (Minnie)
Hinson, James M.
Hinson, Mrs. Joy
Hinson, Marshall
Hinson, Mrs. Patricia
Hodges, Mrs. W. W. (Maggie)
Herring, Stephen
Holder, Mrs. Gordon A. (Anna)
Holland, Felton G.
Holland, Mrs. Vivian
Holland, Mrs. John D. (Ada)
Holland, Mrs. M. C., Jr. (Jean)
Holland, M. C., Sr.
Holland, Mrs. Edna
Holland, Robert Ray
Hood, Mrs. Lillian Adley
Horne, James H.
Hudson, Mrs. Edwin (Olese)
Hudson, M. W. (Kie)
Hudson, Mrs. Lunetie
Hudson, Ralph
Hudson, John
Hudson, David
Hudson, Cindy
Hudson, Rev. Sam F.
Hudson, Mrs. Sam F.
Hudson, William L.

Hudson, Mrs. Patsy
Hudson, Randy
Hudson, Perry
Ingram, John Randolph, II (Randy)
Ingram, Mrs. Kimberly
Jernigan, Mrs. Cecil (Gladys)
Jernigan, Lynn
Jernigan, Glynn
Jernigan, Edward L.
Jernigan, Mrs. Eudell
Jernigan, Harold E.
Jernigan, Mrs. Rowena
Jernigan, Mrs. Luby (Margaret)
Jernigan, Mrs. M. M. (Sallie)
Jernigan, Mrs. W. Robert (Louise)
Johnson, Mrs. Hugh D., Sr. (Shirley)
Johnson, Hugh D., Jr.
Johnson, June
Johnson, Marvin B.
Johnson, Mrs. Dolly
Johnson, Jennifer
Jones, Mrs. Allen E. (Gladys)
Jones, Mrs. Horace (Myrtice)
Jones, J. L., Jr.
Jones, Mrs. Juanita
Jones, O. R. (Bab)
Jones, Mrs. Gladys
Jones, Robert H.
Jones, Mrs. Peggy
Jones, Robert H., Jr.
Jones, Cecil B. (Bo)
Jones, Mrs. Thelma
Jones, Walter E., Jr.
Jones, W. Earl
Jones, Mrs. Frances
Joseph, Nick
Joseph, Charles R.
King, Samuel E.
King, Mrs. Janice
Kinlaw, R. W.
Kinlaw, Mrs. Alice
Kittrell, Leon L., Jr.
Kittrell, Mrs. Laney
Kittrell, Doris
Kyff, Mrs. John (Iris)
Lassiter, Edward
Lassiter, Mrs. Mary
Lassiter, Keen

Lassiter, Mary Leigh
Lawrence, Hylton
Lawrence, Mrs. Phyllis
Lawrence, William P., Jr.
Lawrence, Peggy
Ledford, Mark
Ledford, Poe H.
Ledford, Mrs. Bobbie
Ledford, Carol
Lee, Charles A.
Lee, Mrs. Cecil Ray
Lee, Mrs. Cecil Ray (Sallie)
Lee, Howard M., Sr.
Lee, Mrs. Juanita
Lee, James E.
Lee, Mrs. Carol
Lee, Kenneth
Lee, Mrs. Linda
Lee, Tony R.
Livingston, Mrs. C. C. (Brenda)
Lovelace, William (Bill)
Lovelace, Mrs. Louise
McAdams, Mrs. Selene P.
McCall, Mrs. John R. (Ola)
McKay, John A., Jr.
McLamb, Mrs. D. M. (Fannie)
McLamb, Jimmy
McLamb, Mrs. Virginia
McLamb, Allen
McLeod, Max
McLeod, Mrs. Hazel
Mann, Ivan J., Jr. (Jack)
Mann, Mrs. Katheryn
Mann, Ivanna
Mann, Rhonda
Manning, Mrs. Augusta
Manning, Oliver O.
Manning, Mrs. Gladys
Matthews, Dallas
Matthews, Mrs. Edna
Matthews, Dallas, Jr.
Matthews, Mrs. Betty Jean
Matthews, Miss Evelyn
Matthews, Miss Hazel
Matthews, Miss Ophelia
Maxwell, Mrs. Ethel
Maynard, Mrs. Allie (Sarah)
Maynard, Mrs. L. C. (Ava)

Mitchell, Mrs. Dorothy
Mitchell, Marty
Mitchell, Henry
Mixon, Willard
Mixon, Mrs. Josephine
Mixon, Patricia
Monds, Mrs. Adelaide
Monds, Melissa
Moore, Mrs. Dora
Moore, Sallie Ann
Moore, J. C.
Moore, Mrs. Gene
Moore, Mike
Naylor, Carlyle
Naylor, Luby
Naylor, Mrs. Anna
Naylor, Mrs. Robert (Linda)
Naylor, Mrs. S. R. (Hattie)
Nehring, Mrs. Michael '
Newton, Taylor
Newton, Mrs. Carolyn
Newton, Elizabeth
Newton, Virginia Ann
Norris, Mrs. Gary (Debbie Moore)
Norris, Miss Gertrude
O'Brien, Mrs. Whylma
Overman, Mrs. Ernest L. (Ruth)
Parham, John
Parham, Mrs. Sallie
Parham, Michael (Mike)
Parham, Ronnie
Parker, Mrs. Frank (Jane)
Parker, Allison
Parker, John H.
Parker, Mrs. Mildred
Parker, Phillip
Parrish, Charles Gilmer
Parrish, Mrs. Jean
Peay, Mrs. C. Hubert (Emma)
Phillips, Nathan Ray
Phillips, Virginia (Ginny)
Pittard, Miss Virginia
Pope, Mrs. Alan (Kathy)
Pope, Mrs. Clifford (Gladys)
Pope, Mrs. Grace
Pope, John Henry
Pope, Mrs. Flossie
Pope, Dr. Lloyd A.

Pope, Mrs. Janie
Pope, Lloyd, Jr.
Pope, Ricky T.
Proctor, Mrs. Arthur (Jackie)
Raynor, Mrs. Marvin (Avis)
Raynor, Mrs. Milton
ReBarker, Mrs. Betty D.
Riddle, Noah B.
Riddle, Mrs. Lena
Riddle, Jimmy
Riddle, Randy
Roberts, Mrs. Beatrice
Roberts, Ricky
Roberts, Johnny Ray
Robinette, Miss Madeline
Roebuck, Garland
Roebuck, Mrs. Myrtle
Roebuck, Garland II
Roebuck, Steve
Roseman, Howard
Ruark, Herbert
Ruark, Judy
Ruark, Mrs. Joseph (Emma Ann)
Ryals, Mrs. Henry (Ruby P.)
Ryals, W. E.
Ryals, Mrs. Thelma
Saterfiel, G. T.
Saterfiel, Mrs. Lucy
Saterfiel, Mary Sue
Schwill, Mrs. Caroline
Smith, Miss Fannie Belle
Sinclair, Eric, Sr.
Sinclair, Mrs. Shirley .
Sinclair, Tim
Sinclair, Michael (Mike)
Sinclair, Mrs. Rhonda
Skinner, Charles U.
Skinner, Chas. L. (Pete)
Skinner, Mrs. Glenda
Skinner, Sara
Skinner, Scott
Slaughter, Bennie O.
Slaughter, Mrs. Bertha
Smith, Gordon
Smith, Mrs. Lucille
Smith, J. Nowell, Jr.
Smith, Mrs. Hazel
Smith, Mrs. John R. (Nettie)

Smith, Mrs. Marion
Smith, R. Nowell (Butch)
Smith, Mrs. Beth
Snipes, Larry D.
Snipes, Mrs. Cathy
Snipes, Mrs. Ralph V.
Snow, Dwight W.
Snow, Mrs. Susan
Spears, Wm. David
Spears, Mrs. Jo
Stallings, Mrs. Mary Drake
Stephenson, Mrs. L. Garland
Stevenson, Mrs. Maxine McLeod
Stewart, Mrs. Chas. L. (Bertie)
Stewart, Mrs. Edwin (Frances)
Stewart, Mrs. Sam (Irene)
Stewart, Mrs. W. C. (Louise)
Storey, Mrs. Charles (Rose)
Strickland, H. Paul
Strickland, Mrs. Dee
Strickland, John F.
Strickland, Mrs. Ruby
Strickland, Julius Lanier
Strickland, Mary Louise
Strickland, Charles R.
Strickland, O. Bobby
Strickland, Mrs. Annie Sue
Strickland, Mrs. Paul L., Sr. (Inez)
Strickland, Paul L., Jr.
Strickland, Mrs. Edna Gray
Strickland, Mrs. R. Dennis (Wheatly)
Strickland, R. Dennis, Jr.
Surles, Bruce
Surles, Harper B.
Surles, Mrs. Lennie
Tart, Howard L.
Tart, Mrs. Ruth
Tart, J. Woodrow
Tart, Mrs. Louise
Tart, Mrs. James B. (Neva)
Tart, Earl
Tew, Mrs. Fay Barbour
Thomas, J. I.
Thomas, Mrs. Julia
Thomas, J. Perry
Thomas, Mrs. Opal
Thomas, Larry W.
Thomas, Mrs. Janice

Thomas, Katherine Grey
Thomas, Elizabeth Paige
Thomas, Michael David
Thomas, Mrs. Cashie
Thomas, Richard
Thomas, Mrs. Jane
Thompson, Benjamin N. (Ben)
Thompson, Mrs. Patrice
Thornton, Miss Vara Lee
True, Mrs. Eula
Thomas, Jesse J.
Thomas, Mrs. Gay
Thomas, Andrea
Thomas, Blair
Turlington, Marvin
Turlington, Mrs. Madeline
Turnage, Charles
Turnage, Mrs. Lauralene
Turnage, Steve
Turnage, Mrs. J. Furman (Evelyn)
Tyner, Mrs. J. Harvey (Gertrude)
Upchurch, Mrs. Cad (Nelva)
Wade, Charles C.
Wade, Mrs. Ethel
Wade, Mrs. James L. (Joyce)
Walton, Mrs. Percy (Dorothy)
Walton, Mrs. Fred (Peggy)
Walton, Dawn
Warren, Calvin
Warren, Clifford
Warren, Mrs. Pauline
Warren, Ernest C.
Warren, Mrs. Ollie Grey
Warren, Mrs. George, Sr.
Warren, Miss Foye
Warren, Luby
Warren, Mrs. Agnes
Warren, Luby S.
Warren, Mrs. Catherine
Watkins, Albert F.
Watkins, Mrs. Retha
Watkins, Larry
Watkins, Jerry
Watkins, Mrs. Joyce
Weaver, Robert
Weaver, Mrs. Emily
Weaver, Lou
Weeks, Jesse

Weeks, Mrs. Georgia
Weeks, Ray A.
Weeks, Mrs. Joy
Wells, Robert T. (Bobby)
Wells, Mrs. JoAnn
Wells, Taylor
Wells, Michael Bryan
West, A. L., Sr. (Pete)
West, Mrs. Magdalene
West, Mrs. Charles O. (Juanita)
West, Charles, Jr.
West, John Robert
West, R. A.
West, Mrs. Edna
West, Bobby
Westbrook, Mrs. Earl (Mary)
Westbrook, Mrs. H. A. (Louie Bell
Westbrook, Richard (Sonny)
White, Paul G., Sr.
White, Mrs. Ruth
Whitman, Leon
Whitman, Mrs. Maxine
Whiteman, Mike
White, Mrs. Delores Byrd
White, Miss Melissa
White, Miss Tabatha
Whitehurst, Miss Ann
Whittenton, Mrs. Marjorie
Whittenton, Ben
Whittenton, Mrs. Dewey (Iva)
Whittenton, Henry
Whittenton, Mrs. Reta
Whittenton, Mrs. Virgie
Wiggins, Mrs. Sam (Kate)
Williams, Arthur Franklin
Williams, George, Jr.
Williams, George W., Sr.
Williams, Mrs. Jennie
Williams, Miss Jane
Williams, Scarlette
Williams, Curtis
Williams, Brent
Williams, Craig
Wilson, Mrs. Jesse M.
Wilson, Mrs. J. O (Etta West)
Wilson, Mrs. Joseph (Blanche)
Wilson, Mrs. Oscar T. (Beulah)
Wilson, O. T., Jr.

Wilson, Mrs. Hilda
Woodlief, Mrs. Vivian
Young, Joe
Young, Mrs. Addie

Youngblood, Mrs. Beatrice
Youngblood, Earl
Youngblood, Harold

(The above roster furnished by Church Office and not compiled by this writer)

MEMBERS OF CRESTVIEW MISSION
AS OF August 27, 1981

Allen, Miss Tina N.
Allen, Miss Susan Rene
Ammons, Miss Gail Lee
Bryant, Mrs. Patricia S.
Byrd, Mr. Bobby Lynn
Beasley, Mrs. Janice
Beasley, Mr. Woody Keith
Baggett, Mrs. Catherine Faircloth
Baucom, Miss Mary Elizabeth
Brown, Mrs. W. R. (Betty)
Baucom, Miss Angela Marie
Barker, Mrs. Ethel
Barker, Mr. D. F.
Dowd, Leonard Eugene
Eason, Mr. Scottie Lane
Fann, Mrs. James A. (Mary Lee)
Gilbert, Mr. James Richard
Godwin, Mrs. Barbara
Guin, Mrs. Mickey Angela Bass
House, Miss Tammy Lynn
House, Miss Anita Lynette
House, Miss Ann Michelle
House, Mrs. Ruth Helen McLeod
Hall, Mrs. Shelby Gray
Hodgeman, Mr. Rodney M.
Hodgeman, Mrs. Dorothy Jean
Hodgeman, Mr. Douglas Scott
Hodgeman, Miss Sonia
Jernigan, Miss Annette
Jernigan, Mr. Donnie Ray
Jernigan, Mrs. Pat (Donnie Ray)
Jernigan, Mrs. Barbara
Jernigan, Mr. Hubert Owen
Jernigan, Miss Teresa Lynn
Jernigan, Miss Peggy Sue
Jernigan, Miss Debbie

Lee, Mr. Bassie
Lee, Mrs. Pearl
Lee, Mr. Larry Leon
Lee, Miss Tammy Malinda
McPherson, Mr. C. Michael (Mike)
McPherson, Mrs. C. Michael (Frances)
Morgan, Mrs. Lois
Norris, Mrs. Faye
Oldham, Mr. Henry Lee
Oldham, Mrs. Henry Lee
Oldham, Miss Teresa Gail
Pipkin, Milton
Pipkin, Mrs. Milton (Roena)
Sutton, Mr. Christopher Bryan
Sutton, Mrs. Jo Ann
Sutton, Miss Le-Ann
Sutton, Mr. Rodney, Jr.
Stewart, Mrs. Dorothy Anne
Stanley, Mrs. Gladys Fay
Stancil, Mrs. Janice
Tart, Mr. James David
Tart, Mrs. James David (Brenda W.)
Tart, Mr. James Andrew
Tart, Mrs. James Carl (Oleda Blanch)
Tart, Mr. James Carl
Tart, Mr. Raeford
Tart, Mrs. Raeford L. (Virginia)
Tart, Mrs. Joyce Mae
West, Mr. Otis (deceased)
West, Mrs. Vennie
Westbrook, Mr. Lloyd Harold
Westbrook, Mrs. Linda Lou
Westbrook, Miss Linda Joyce
West, Mrs. Mary
West, Mrs. Wilma
Wilson, Mrs. Mary Lou

(The above roster furnished by Church Office and not compiled by this writer)

Adcock, Charles
Addison, Mrs. Rufus R.
Alabaster, Vickie
Aldinger, Robert Frederic
Alford, Mrs. Francis Tart
Altman, Coleman
Ammons, Miss Virginia
Anderson, Cecil
Atkins, Virginia Dare
Baker, James V.
Baker, Mrs. James V. (Doris)
Barnes, J. D.
Barnes, Mrs. J. D. (Henrietta)
Bailey, Frank, Jr.
Bailey, Hazel
Baird, Miss Viola
Baker, James
Barefoot, Kay Frances
Barrier, Mrs. William Smith
    (Alma Belle)
Barrow, Mrs. Mary
Batts, Billy
Bennett, Mrs. Margaret Rayfield
Beechum, Carol Sue
Bethea, Ralph
Blackburn, J. A.
Black, Mrs. Callie Price
Blackley, O. P.
Blackwell, Mrs. Dale, Jr.
    (Norma Jean)
Bowman, Richard
Brannan, Wade M., Jr.
Brewer, Edwin Ray
Brock, Billy
Brown, Betty Elizabeth
Brown, Trissie Ellen
Buchannan, Miss Mary
Burch, Mrs. Esther Morgan
Bush, Ruth
Butler, Eugene
Cheek, C. R.
Cheek, Mrs. C. R. (Beulah)
Clayton, Elbert T.
Clayton, Mrs. Myrtis Yancey
Cain, Fred

Cain, Mrs. Fred
Campbell, Miss Virginia
Carr, James Owen
Chalk, Wilbur
Chalk, Mrs. Wilbur
Coats, Leonard Edward
Coats, Rose Marie
Colville, Mrs. Larry T. (Kathryn)
Cook, Mrs. Fred
Cresswell, R. S.
Cresswell, Mrs. R. A.
Cullom, Miss Ernestine
Dalrymple, John, Jr.
Dalrymple, Mary Sue
Daniels, Dexter
Daniels, James
Daniels, Leonard
Dawson, Mack
Deal, Betty Lou
Dixon, Roy Danny
Dixon, Grace S.
Dudley, Ray
Duncan, Oliver C., Jr.
Early, Carolyn
Elliott, Mrs. Frank (Vada)
Ennis, Earl
Eubanks, W. A.
Freeman, Mrs. Frank
    (Nine Alice)
Fries, Mrs. Bob (Dorothy)
Godwin, Mr. Ronald Lane
Gainey, Dorothy Jean
Gardner, David
Giles, Mrs. Jackie Jernigan
Glover, Fleming
Glover, Sue Early
Godwin, Lewis, Jr.
Godwin, Joe
Godwin, Herman, Jr.
Godwin, Mrs. Homer Patrick
    (Nancy)
Glover, Mrs. Fleming J.
    (Marjorie)
Harrell, James W.

Harrell, Mrs. James W.
    (Shirley)
Harrington, Mrs. DeWitt
    (Hariett)
Herring, Anne Hall
Haithcox, J. D.
Hall, A. L. Clem
Hall, A. Roland
Hall, Mary
Hall, Mrs. Ruby
Hall, William Anderson
Harden, Mrs. Eugene
    (Joyce Pope)
Hardison, David A., Jr.
Hardison, Sandra
Hardison, Mrs. Sherrill
    (Patricia Ann)
Hawley, Mrs. David
    (Ellen)
Hayden, Mrs. Anna Smith
Hazeldon, Mrs. O. B.
    (Verda Jernigan)
Hendricks, Mrs. W. O.
    (Denella)
Herring, Bishop
Hinnant, Mrs. P. L.
Hinton, Roy
Hodges, Eugene
Holland, Charles Wallace
Holland, Herbert Dare
Holler, Mrs. Richard Louis
    (Gloria Barnes)
Honeycutt, Donald
Hopkins, Michael
House, Mrs. R. W.
Ivey, Joyce
Johnson, Ralph, Jr.
Jernigan, Miss Janet
Jackson, Mrs. Charles
    (Carolyn Gardner)
Jackson, Mrs. B. J.
    (Barbara Martin)
Jackson, Edna Mae
Jackson, Grace Lee
Jackson, Gloria Jean
Jackson, Miss Glenda
Jackson, Howell
Jackson, Hugh

Jernigan, Mrs. J. T.
Jernigan, Walter
Johnson, Amos C.
Johnson, Mrs. Amos
    (Judith)
Johnson, Bobbie
Johnson, Mrs. Clemuel
    (Nancy Sugg)
Johnson, Douglas
Johnson, E. B., Jr.
Johnson, Mrs. James
Jones, Carr
Jones, O. C.
Jones, Mrs. O. C.
Jones, W. Paul
Keene, I. W., Jr.
Kirby, Kenneth N.
Langdon, Mrs. Talmage H.
Lee, Betty Lou
Lee, Howard M., Jr.
Lee, Mrs. John Mack
    (Jewell Holland)
Lee, Harry Kline
Lee, Carl
Lee, Clel E.
Lewis, Mrs. Charles
Lewis, Mrs. Tommy
    (Marth Ann)
Lynch, Francis
McDonald, Mrs. Bleese
McLamb, Cindy
McLamb, Mrs. Jean Martin
McLamb, Theodore
Moss, John C.
Moss, Mrs. John C.
Moss, John Richard
Moss, Robert Neal
Manning, Richard
Mason, Charles F.
Mason, Mrs. Charles F.
Matthews, Mrs. David
Mitchell, Mrs. Mamie
Monds, Richard S., Jr.
Monds, Mrs. Cindy
Moore, Miss Inez
Morgan, Haxel
Murphy, James L.

Murphy, Mrs. James L.
  (Madaline)
Murphy, Patrick Michael
Murphy, Sheila Ann
Murray, Mrs. Ocie F.
  (Debroah Josephine)
Norris, Miss Inez
Naylor, Ammie
Newell, Patty
Norris, Miss Ada Frances
Norris, Mrs. Mann, Jr.
  (Erline)
Norris, Stonewall
Nowell, Mrs. Tal E.
Owens, Henry L.
Pope, Mrs. Willis
Pope, Frances
Palpant, Mrs. Pierre Rene
  (Elaine)
Partin, Mrs. Leo
  (Blanch Gainey)
Parrish, Lois
Parrish, Betty Larue
Paschal, Mrs. Eva
Pearce, Mrs. Evan Oris, III
  (Isabelle Naylor)
Peay, Jimmy
Phillips, Mrs. J. T.
Phillips, James Harold
Pollard, Mrs. Tillman
Pope, Joyce Faye
Price, Raymond
Price, Mrs. Raymond
Price, Robert L.
Price, Mrs. Robert L.
Page, Robert A.
Raines, Mrs. William Nordan
Rayfield, M. B.
Rayfield, Mrs. M. B.
Rayford, H. I.
Raynor, Milton, Jr.
Reeves, Charles Daniel
Reeves, Mrs. Charles Daniel
  (Barbara)
Riddle, Teresa
Roth, Mrs. Arthur, Jr.
  (Becky Aycock)
Royals, Miss Marie

Russell, Clyde Hayworth
Rollins, Mrs. Cora Leigh
Ryals, Wesley
Ryals, Donald
Sabastian, Ron
Sabastian, Mrs. Revonda
Salmon, Hilary Conner
Slamon, Mrs. Hilary C.
Shelton, Alma Lee
Sherrill, Joe
Sills, Mrs. Linwood Hugh
  (Effie Lou)
Sills, Mrs. Hubert L.
Smith, Mrs. D. W.
Smith, Mrs. Earl
  (Rhetta McLamb)
Smith, Mrs. Ray (Jo Ann)
Spence, Mrs. Wallace A.
  (Elese Gainey)
Stephens, Mrs. Eula Butler
Stephens, Judson
Stephenson, Colon, Jr.
Stewart, Keith Dudley
Stewart, Mrs. Olin T.
Stewart, H. L.
Stewart, Miss Polly
Stinson, B. C.
Stinson, Mrs. B. C.
Strickland, Norma Grey
Sturgill, Jackie
Suggs, Mrs. Everett S.
Sugg, Mary Sue
Summer, Mrs. Toby (Sue)
Swan, Mrs. Tommie
Tart, Corbett W.
Tart, John
Taylor, Sandra
Tew, Mrs. Henry
  (Pansy Lowery)
Thomas, Mrs. Darius M.
Thomas, Eddie
Thomas, Lois Pauline
Thomason, Mrs. Gilbert
  (Jane Westbrook)
Thornton, Billy
Thornton, LeRoy
Tomberlie, Mrs. Calvin
  (Trudy)

Turlington, Mrs. Silas	Warren, Marie
Underwood, Mrs. Fleet M.	West, Mrs. Adele J.
Underwood, Sarah	Williamson, I. J., Sr.
Van Harlingen, Mrs. Jewel Harris	Williamson, I. J., Jr.
Wade, Ronnie	Wilson, Edward Holt
Warren, Major William Howard	Williams, Mrs. Maxine Parrish
Winfield, Mrs. Linda	Wishart, Mrs. David
Wall, Mrs. Clarence	Wrench, Mrs. Rosa Lee
(Jewel McLean)	Yancey, Mrs. W. F.
Wallace, Mrs. William	Yancey, Miss Charlotte
Warren, Connie H.	Yancey, Miss Mae

(This writer recognizes that errors may exist in this Roster of Non-Resident Members. However it is the best information available to him at this time.)

CONSTITUTION
OF
THE FIRST BAPTIST CHURCH OF DUNN, NORTH CAROLINA

PREAMBLE

For the purpose of preserving, propagating and making known specifically the principles of our Faith, and to the end that this body of believing Christians may be governed in an orderly manner consistant with the accepted principals of Missionary Baptist Churches, for the purpose of preserving the liberties inherent in each individual member of the church, and in order to set forth the relationship of this body to other Baptist bodies, we do adopt and establish this Constitution.

ARTICLE I. NAME

The name of this organization shall be The First Baptist Church of Dunn, North Carolina.

ARTICLE II. PURPOSE

The First Baptist Church of Dunn is organized for the purpose of advancing and promoting the worship of God through the reading and study of the Holy Bible as the revealed word of God, the teaching and preaching of the Gospel of our Lord and Savior, Jesus Christ, conducting regular services of worship for the spirtual training, development and benefit of each member and for the winning of souls to Jesus Christ. This church shall be missionary in spirit, extending the Gospel through our organized religious channels to the entire world. It shall promote and maintain the teachings and doctrines of that Christian denomination universally known and designated as the Missionary Baptist Denomination. It shall exist to provide regular opportunities for public worship, to sustain the ordinances, doctrines and ethics set forth in the New Testament for the church of our Lord Jesus Christ, and to channel its offerings to the support of the objects of the Kingdom of God. In order to effectively carry forward the objects and purposes set forth above, the Church will have full power and authority to purchase, lease and acquire by gift, devise or bequest and to hold, mortgage, convey and dispose of all kinds of property, both real and personal.

ARTICLE III. MEMBERSHIP

SECTION 1. COMPOSITION OF PRESENT MEMBERSHIP

The membership of this Church shall be composed of persons whose names appear on the roll of this Church at the date of the adoption of this Constitution.

SECTION 2. RECEPTION OF NEW MEMBERS

Members may be received in this Church in the following ways:

A. By vote of the Church after a candidate has given evidence of regeneration by the spirit of God and following the baptism of such candidate by immersion.

B. A member of another Church may be received by a vote of the Church upon promise of letter of transfer from the church where membership resides, provided such member has been baptised by immersion. If such person has not been baptised by immersion, such person's membership shall be effective following such baptism. The applying member will be in a watch-care relationship until letter of transfer is received from the other church.

C. Anyone who has once been a member of a Baptist Church and in consequence of peculiar circumstances has lost that relationship or is not able otherwise to promise a letter of transfer may be received into the fellowship of this Church upon statement to the membership of faith and previous baptism by immersion and by a vote of the Church.

D. Application for membership under circumstances other than those described in A, B and C above will be considered by the Church in conference and the decision of the Church will be final in each case.

SECTION 3. TERMINATION OF MEMBERSHIP

Membership shall be terminated in the following ways:

A. A letter of transfer to unite with another Baptist Church may be issued, upon request, to the church in which the member is planning to join, providing such member is in good standing. All such applications must be passed upon by the Church in conference.

B. A member's name shall be dropped from the roll of membership at the time of this death.

C. Any member's name shall be removed from the Church roll upon the written request of such member to the effect that he desires his name to be so removed.

D. A member's name shall be removed from the roll upon it becoming known that such member has become affiliated with a church of another faith or denomination.

E. The Church, after due notice and opportunity for hearing, and every possible kindly effort to make such action unnecessary, may upon majority of vote, terminate the membership of a person in this body for reasons it considers sufficient to warrant such action.

SECTION 4. DUTIES OF MEMBERS

Members are expected to be faithful in all of the duties essential to the Christian life; to attend regularly the services of the Church; to give regularly and systematically to its support and Kingdom causes; and to share in its organized work.

ARTICLE IV. MEETINGS

SECTION 1. This Church shall hold regular meetings for worship, teaching, training and fellowship.

SECTION 2. This Church shall hold regular business meetings for the disposition of all business matters not otherwise provided for, to hear reports from the various church organizations and to consider other matters essential to the spiritual welfare and prosperity of the congregation. Notice of such business meetings shall be given in the Church publications and or at a regular meeting at least one week in advance.

SECTION 3. Other meetings of the Church as a whole or of authorized groups within the Church may be set according to the needs of the congregation.

ARTICLE V. OFFICERS

The officers of this Church shall be a pastor, and other vocational leadership as needed, deacons, trustees, clerk, treasurer, and such other officers as shall be required to do the work of the Church in any of its departments or organizations. All of these shall be elected by the Church and shall be members in good standing at the time of election except that a pastor may not be a member until after his call.

ARTICLE VI. ELECTION AND DUTIES OF CHURCH OFFICERS

A. Pastor

SECTION 1 Call: Whenever a vacancy occurs, a pastor shall be called by the Church to serve until the relationship is dissolved at the request of either the pastor or the Church. In either case, at least sixty days' notice shall be given of termination of the relationship, unless otherwise mutually agreed upon, with both pastor and Church seeking to follow the will of God through the leadership of the Holy Spirit.

The Church may, however, terminate the relationship in shorter time provided pastor's salary be continued through the sixty day period.

The call of the pastor shall take place at a meeting especially set for that purpose of which at least one week's notice has been given the membership. The election shall be upon the recommendation of a special committee recommended by the deacons and approved by the Church to seek out and nominate as pastor a minister of the gospel whose Christian character and qualifications fit him for the office. The committee shall bring only one name at a time for the consideration of the Church and no nominations shall be made except by the committee. Election shall be by standing vote or by ballot at the discretion of the congregation with an affirmative vote of three-fourths of those present and voting necessary for an extension of a call. Should the minister recommended by the committee fail to receive a three-fourths vote, the committee will be instructed to seek out another minister and the meeting at which the vote was taken shall be adjourned without debate.

SECTION 2. Duties: The pastor shall have in charge the welfare and oversight of the Church; he shall be ex-officio member of all organizations, departments and committees; he may call a special meeting of the deacons or of any committee according to procedures which are set forth in the By-Laws; he shall conduct religious services on stated and on special occasions, administer the ordinances, minister to the spiritual needs of the members of the Church and community; he shall perform other duties that usually pertain to that office; he shall have special charge of the pulpit ministry of the Church and shall, in cooperation with the Pulpit

Committee and/or the Deacons, provide for pulpit supply when he is absent, and shall arrange, with the concurrence of the pulpit committee, for ministers to assist in revival meetings and workers to assist in other special services required by the Church. It shall be his special responsibility to win the lost to Christ, to minister to the spiritual needs of the members of his congregation, and through prayer and study to render effective preaching and pastoral ministries.

B. Deacons

The Active Diaconate shall consist of thirty Deacons, male or female, plus any Lifetime Deacons. Deacons shall be elected from among those Church members who have proven themselves to have Scriptural qualifications according to I Timothy 3 and Titus I. They shall be elected for a term of three years. After serving a three year term, Deacons shall retain their title of Deacon and may be called upon for service by the Church at any time but shall be ineligible for re-election to the Active Diaconate until at least one year has elapsed following their retirement from this service.

The Deacons presently serving shall continue to serve for the term to which they were elected. Annually, on or before September 1st, the Church, as a whole, shall nominate from a list of the Adult Church membership at least two members for each vacancy occurring on the Active Diaconate for the forthcoming year and a list of such nominations shall be presented to the Church for a vote for the purpose of reducing the number of nominees to twice the number of vacancies occuring for the forthcoming year and any vacancies existing as a result of death, resignation or any other reason. The individuals receiving the highest number of votes shall be the nominees. Vote shall be by secret ballot. In the event of a tie vote, the list of nominees shall be increased by the number of such individuals involved in the tie vote determining the maximum number of nominees as heretofore provided. No person is eligible for nomination to a term which will result in such person serving at the same time such person's spouse has been previously elected to serve. In the event that husband and wife both receive sufficient votes for nomination, that spouse receiving the lesser number of votes will be disqualified as a nominee.

The annual election to fill the vacancies in the Active Diaconate shall be held on the third Sunday in September. Election shall be by secret written ballot. Those ten nominees receiving the highest number of votes shall be declared elected to a full term. The nominees receiving the next highest number of votes shall be declared elected to any unexpired term vacancies with the nominees receiving the higher number of votes being elected to the vacancies with the longest remaining term of service. In the event of ties those nominees involved shall be submitted to the Church for election by secret written ballot on the fourth Sunday in September.

The vote shall be counted by a Counting Committee comprised of Deacons whose term is expiring on the 1st day of October of the current year, with the Chairperson of the Counting Committee being the Chairperson of the Active Diaconate, if such person qualifies for the Counting Committee, but if such person fails to qualify then the Chairperson of such committee shall be appointed by the Chairperson of the Active Diaconate from among such qualified persons.

Each newly elected Deacon must be ordained by the Church in a regular worship service. The pastor will provide leadership and direct the service. Following ordination all newly elected Deacons shall be installed into the body of Deacons.

Newly elected Deacons shall take office as of the 1st day of October, at which time the terms of the Deacons which they succeed expire.

Lifetime Deacons are Deacons elected as such by the Church in conference by the majority of the members present following nomination by the Active Diaconate.

A Lifetime Deacon is an officer of the Church who has distinguished himself or herself in Christian service. Lifetime Deacons shall have the same rights and privileges, including voting rights, as members of the Active Diaconate.

The regular meeting of the Active Diaconate shall be held on the second Monday of each month unless otherwise changed by a vote of the Active Diaconate.

The Active Diaconate shall elect annually by secret written ballot, following nominations from the floor, at the first regular meeting following the annual election of Deacons, a Chairperson, a Vice-Chairperson and a Secretary to serve for one year or until replaced by vote of the Active Diaconate.

Deacons shall at all times regard themselves as servants of the Church. With the pastor, and as the Holy Spirit may direct, they are to consider and make recommendations to the Church in all matters pertaining to its Work and progress, including oversight of the discipline of the Church and establishment and maintenance of spiritual fraternal relations with all members of the Church. They shall assist the pastor in the observance of the ordinances; have general oversight over the upkeep, repair and use of property (with proper respect for the responsibilities of the Church trustees), supervise the financial program of the Church. They shall arrange for regular meetings and such committees as are necessary to the discharge of their duties. The pastor, or the chairperson of the deacons, may call the deacons into special session whenever need for such arises.

C. Trustees

For the Church year beginning October 1, 1978 there shall be three persons elected to serve as trustees. Persons now serving as trustees shall serve until these trustees are duly elected by the Church in conference. At all times there shall be three trustees who are to hold in trust all Church property for the benefit of those members of the Church who adhere and submit to the regular order of the Church and who follow the established usages, customs, doctrines, practices and organization of the Church, together with its connections with other denominational bodies whether a majority or a minority of the membership. The trustees shall execute all contracts, deeds, mortgages or other instruments when authorized to do so by the Church in conference. The trustees shall serve for an indefinite term and until their successors are duly elected by the Church in conference. Upon the death, resignation, or inability to serve by any of the trustees a successor shall be elected by the Church in a conference called for this purpose.

D. Clerk

The clerk shall be elected annually upon recommendation of whatever committee is established to recommend the Church officers. It shall be his responsibility to attend or be represented at all church business meetings, to keep an accurate record of all business transactions, to prepare the annual associational letter and to see that it is properly transmitted to the associational clerk, and he shall notify all officers, members of committees and messengers of their election or appointment; he shall issue letters of dismission as authorized by the Church, preserve all papers and valuable records and letters that belong to the Church, and preserve a true history of the Church, keeping same in a safe place. It shall be the duty of the clerk to see that an accurate roll of the church membership is kept, the dates and methods of admission and dismissal, change in name, correct mailing address and other pertinent information about each member.

E. Treasurer

The Church shall elect a treasurer annually. One who has served previously in this position will be eligible for re-election. It shall be the duty of the treasurer to receive, keep in a bank, and disburse by check upon proper authority all money or things of value that are given to the Church in accordance with instructions from the Church. He shall keep at all times an itemized account of all receipts and disbursements; rendering an account regularly to the Church to be preserved by the church clerk. The treasurer's books shall be audited at least once a year as arranged by the Church, and all books, records and accounts kept by him shall be the property of the Church. The treasurer shall upon invitaticᵣ meet with the deacons, and shall be an ex-officio member of the Finance Committee and of the Budget Committee.

ARTICLE VII. CHURCH GOVERNMENT

SECTION 1. The government of this Church shall be congregational in nature and shall be vested in the membership.

SECTION 2. Church Conference: A church conference shall be held on Wednesday night of each month following the regular meeting on the deacons and at such other times as may be necessary. In addition to stated conferences, a conference of the Church may be called at any time by the pastor and chairperson or deacons, or upon the request of the Church.

SECTION 3. Moderator: The pastor or chairperson of deacons shall preside over church conference as moderator. In their absence the vice-chairperson of the deacons shall preside and in such person's absence, the chairperson of the deacons shall name some other member of the Church in Good standing to assume this responsibility.

SECTION 4. Quorum: A quorum shall consist of not less than five percent of the adult members of the Church, except for the election or dismissal of Church officers or amendment to the Church Constitution, ten percent. For the call or dismissal of a pastor, twenty-five percent of the adult members of the Church shall be necessary to constitute a quorum.

Section 5. Minutes: The church clerk shall keep minutes of each business meeting and shall record the approximate number present, whether a quorum present and what actions were taken by the Church.

SECTION 6. Vote: Any vote provided for by this Constitution shall be only by those members present at the time such vote is called for.

ARTICLE VIII. AFFILIATION

SECTION 1. This Church is a free, autonomous, independent body, congregational in nature with authority to determine for itself in the manner set forth in this Constitution, free of any outside control, authority or power, whether governmental or otherwise, the use of its property and all church policies.

SECTION 2. Association: The Church recognizes the value and mutual helpfulness in the voluntary association of churches which are in such agreement in faith and practice as to make possible a spirit of fellowship and good will. It is recognized that association and cooperation between such churches will influence the missionary, educational and benevolent interest of each other. The Church does, therefore, declare its intention as far as conscience will allow to work in mutual cooperation with other Baptist groups.

SECTION 3. Affiliation: Upon the adoption of this Constitution this Church shall be deemed to have affiliated itself with the Little River Baptist Association.

SECTION 4. Cooperation: Upon adoption of this Constitution this Church shall be deemed to be in friendly cooperation with the aims and purposes of the Baptist State Convention of North Carolina and of the Southern Baptist Convention as set forth in the Constitution of these autonomous bodies and through duly elected messengers will participate in their deliberative assemblies, and shall as we are able, support the missionary, benevolent and educational programs of each.

SECTION 5. Discontinuance of Affiliation and/or Cooperation. The calling of a church conference for the purpose of voting on withdrawal from affiliation from the Little River Baptist Association and/or discontinuance of cooperation with the Baptist State Convention and/or the Southern Baptist Convention will require that written notice be sent to each resident member of the Church, stating the purpose and time of said conference. Action to withdraw to be valid must be carried by vote of two-thirds of the members present and voting; in which cause transferral of property shall be effected in accordance with the will of the two-thirds majority. In the event of serious rupture in fellowship at this point and the necessity of such action as above set forth, it is expected that the various factions of the Church will sit down in Christian love and in the spirit of prayer and seek to effectuate reconciliation of an agreeable basis of division, each being mindful of the Beatitude which says, "Blessed are the peacemakers, for they shall be called sons of God."

ARTICLE IX. ADOPTION AND AMENDMENTS

SECTION 1. This Constitution shall be considered adopted and in immediate effect if and when two-thirds of the members present at the business meeting at which vote is taken shall vote in favor of same. This vote shall be taken not less than thirty days after formal presentation of the Constitution to the Church, and notice of such meeting in which the vote is to be taken shall be given at least one week in advance.

SECTION 2. This Constitution may be amended, altered or repealed by a two-thirds vote of the members present at any regular business meeting of the Church; provided, however, that such amendment, alteration or repeal shall have been given to the clerk in writing; and the proposed change shall have been presented to the Church at least thirty days prior to the time the vote is taken.

BY-LAWS

ARTICLE I. MEETINGS

The Church shall hold regular services of worship on Sundays and Wednesday evenings unless otherwise agreed upon by the Church. The Lord's Supper shall be observed at least once a quarter at a time approved by the Church.

ARTICLE II. OTHER CHURCH OFFICERS

SECTION 1. All church officers subject to annual election shall be elected during the month of September.

SECTION 2. In addition to those named in the body of the Constitution, other officers of the Church shall be a Financial Secretary, Sunday School Director, Training Union Director, President of the Brotherhood, Director of the Woman's Missionary Union, Minister of Education, Minister of Music, Pianist, Organist, and such other officers as may be necessary and desirable. All officers of the Church and its organizations, unless otherwise specified, shall be elected for a term of one year, and upon the recommendation of the Nominating Committee, it being understood, of course, that members of the Church may offer substitute nominations for any position for which the Nominating Committee makes nominations.

ARTICLE III. DUTIES OF CHURCH OFFICERS

SECTION 1. Minister of Education. The Minister of Education shall assist the pastor in the administration of the Church program, with involvement in worship, visitation and other duties. Shall formulate and implement a strong church school program in cooperation with the Sunday School Director, approved and supported by the Church; Shall formulate and implement a strong church training program in cooperation with the Training Union Director, approved and supported by the Church; Shall assist in developing plans and programs to more actively involve the youth in the functions and activities of the Church. Shall assist in developing programs and activities to aid and strengthen other organizations of the church; Shall encourage and assist in developing such other programs and activities as would increase and enlarge the outreach, growth and effectiveness of the Church.

SECTION 2. Minister of Music. The Minister of Music shall be responsible for providing worshipful music at all services. He (or she) is to train and direct the choir, or choirs, and is to cooperate with the pastor and other church leaders in the selection of suitable music, and the devising of appropriate musical programs for all occasions where such services are needed.

SECTION 3. Financial Secretary. The Financial Secretary shall receive the empty offering envelopes after the money has been removed and counted by the proper person(s); and from these he shall give each contributor individual credit as provided in the record system approved by the Church. He shall keep the envelopes for references as the Church directs. He shall keep record of the receipts from envelopes, plate or loose, and miscellaneous or special offering. The Financial Secretary shall also be responsible for preparing and mailing regular statements to all contributing members as the Church directs.

SECTION 4. Sunday School Director. The Director of the Sunday School shall have general oversight of the entire school, and shall administer its affairs in cooperation with, and according to, the plans and methods of the Sunday School Board of the Southern Baptist Convention, subject to the approval of the local Church. He shall acquaint himself with the best methods of religious education and endeavor to adopt them in this school.

It shall be his duty to counsel weekly or monthly with his teachers and officers through officers' and teachers' meetings giving advice and receiving suggestions from his co-workers.

He shall see that a full and accurate report is made of the work of the Sunday School in the regular business meetings of the Church.

SECTION 5. Training Union Director. The Training Union Director shall have charge of the activities of the Training Union. He shall acquaint himself with the program and methods outlined by the Sunday School Board of the Southern Baptist Convention for this organization and shall endeavor to adopt such programs in this Church, subject to the approval of the Church. He shall see that a full and accurate report is given at the regular business meetings of the Church.

SECTION 6. President of the Brotherhood. The President of the Brotherhood shall promote the work of the Brotherhood as outlined by the Brotherhood Commission of the Southern Baptist Convention, seeking to enlist the men of the church in an active program for Christ. He shall see that a full and accurate report is given at the regular business meetings of the Church.

SECTION 7. Director of the Woman's Missionary Union. The Director of the Woman's Missionary Union shall seek to enlist the girls and women of the Church in a program of missionary training, giving, and activity according to plans promoted by the Woman's Missionary Union, Auxiliary to the Southern Baptist Convention. She shall see that a full and accurate report is given at the regular business meetings of the Church.

SECTION 8. Pianist. The Pianist shall play for public services and shall assist the Minister of Music in a suitable program of music for the Church.

SECTION 9. Organist. The Organist shall play for public services and shall assist the Minister of Music in a suitable program of music for the Church.

ARTICLE IV. COMMITTEES AND COUNCILS

SECTION 1. Standing Committees and Councils. The Church shall elect such standing committees and councils as may be deemed necessary to carry out the various phases of the program of the Church efficiently and effectively. In any event, the Church shall have at all times the following standing committees: Nominating, Budget and Finance, Building Maintenance, Grounds Maintenance, Personnel, Baptism, Lord's Supper, Music, Library, Ushers, Flowers, Transportation, Publicity, Missions, Church Ministries, Food Service, Radio and Visual Aids, Literature, Recreation, Forward Program, Nursery Correlating, Youth Activities, Cub

Scouts and any additional committees and councils deemed necessary for the proper function of the Church.

SECTION 2. Temporary Committees. The Church upon recommendation by the deacons may elect at any time committees to perform temporary functions.

SECTION 3. Nominating Committee. The Nominating Committee previously elected by the Church and presently serving shall make nominations for the church year beginning October 1, 1978. For Church years subsequent to the Church year beginning October 1, 1978, the Pastor and Chairperson, Vice-Chairperson, and Secretary of the Active Diaconate together shall appoint two men and two women, designating one of them as chairperson to serve as the nucleus of the Nominating Committee. They in turn shall select nominees for Sunday School Director, Training Union Director, President of the Brotherhood and Director of the Woman's Missionary Union. Names of the nominees shall be placed before the Church for election in June of each year. (Nominations from the floor shall not be precluded.) Upon election, these four officers shall, together with the above mentioned nucleus and the Chairperson of the Active Diaconate, form the Nominating Committee to nominate and present to the Church all other officers, committees and councils of the Church, except as otherwise provided for by this Constitution. The Nominating Committee shall designate one person as chairperson of each committee or council. One half of the nucleus shall rotate off each year. The Pastor, Chairperson of the Active Diaconate and Secretary of the Active Diaconate together shall make appointments to fill all vacancies occuring in the nucleus, making certain that there are always two men and two women in the group, that none succeeds himself or herself, and that a Chairperson is designated each year. The Pastor of the Church shall be an ex-officio member of the Nominating Committee. The committee shall serve throughout the year to fill all vacancies that occur.

ARTICLE V. ADOPTION AND AMENDMENTS

SECTION 1. These By-Laws shall be considered adopted and in immediate effect if and when a majority of the members present at the business meeting at which vote is taken shall vote in favor of same. This vote shall be taken not less than thirty days after formal presentation of the By-Laws to the Church.

SECTION 2. These By-Laws may be amended, altered or repealed by a majority vote of the members present at any regular business meeting of the Church, provided, however,